# THE HEBREW PHILOSOPHICAL GENIUS
## A VINDICATION

D1542879

# THE HEBREW
# PHILOSOPHICAL GENIUS

## A VINDICATION

❦

*By* DUNCAN BLACK MACDONALD, M.A., D.D.

*"For Life is no empty sport, nor were the creatures
formed uncontrolled, although their doings may
not go aright."—Ibn al-Fárid's Greater Tá'íya Ode.*

*NEW YORK*
RUSSELL & RUSSELL · INC
1965

To
Reynold Alleyne Nicholson, F.B.A.
orientalist, philosopher, theologian
for long friendship and in deep respect

# PREFACE

THIS *book, considered on one side, is a supplement to my* The Hebrew Literary Genius, *expanding the two chapters there on Philosophy and on Ecclesiastes. It is, therefore, to be taken with my former book and presupposes that book; of necessity it repeats certain elements but it does so from a different angle. For it is, also, on another side, an attack on a widely prevalent dogma that the Hebrews had no philosophy, being by their very nature incapable of philosophy. That prejudice I have already attacked in my former book, but here I endeavor to expand the attack and, still more, to express it in such philosophical terms as will appeal to those trained in philosophical method. This book, in consequence, cannot be as simple as I tried, at least, to make my first. There are technical terms in it and abstract ideas and even, of necessity, Greek quotations. These I have translated, for I am fully aware that the* Graecum est; non legitur *of the medieval world has returned.*

*In basis and method my attack is twofold. First, I endeavor to show that the Hebrews had fundamental philosophical ideas and attitudes; that these were theirs from their beginnings; and that the more formal expression of these, reached in such later books as Job, Proverbs, Ecclesiastes and Ecclesiasticus, came by an orderly development from such beginnings. This is directed against the very common view that the writers of these later books had come under Greek influence and had been affected by Greek philosophy. That view is largely based upon a feeling that from the conquests of Alexander onwards the Hebrews must have come under that influence and been so affected. We may admit that it is quite possible that some Hebrews may have been so affected, but, on such an a priori argument, no more than that can be said. And my endeavor is to show that those Palestinian Hebrews, whose writings we have, were not so affected. But, secondly, I endeavor to show what actually did happen to Hebrew thinkers when they did come into contact with Greek thought. The Alexandrine Jewish writings are plainly soaked in such thought, both as to vocabulary and ideas.*

*In consequence the conception of the personality of Jehovah held by some of them is entirely changed; no old Hebrew would recognize in the God of Philo the Jehovah of the Old Testament or even the God of Job or Ecclesiastes. This varies, of course, with the different writers. The Greek influence is unmistakable on them all, but Philo, for example, has been led into much stranger speculations and hypotheses than the author of "Wisdom." The author of "Wisdom" may have somewhat spiritualized the Jehovah of the Old Testament and certainly softened the crass nationalism of the Jewish people, but his God is recognizably Jehovah. He brought out the full implication in that unique personality. The ideas of Philo, on the other hand, must have deeply shocked his Palestinian contemporaries, and we know that they were bitterly opposed by one Jewish element in Alexandria.*

*But there is another side of Hebrew thinking which the present book tries to bring out into clearness and the later influence of which it tries to trace. It is the conception of Reason as an entity and person by itself—Herself the Hebrews would have said, present at the creation of the world, possessed by Jehovah but not produced by Him; in reality a coeternal Being with Jehovah. The precise Hebrew origin of this conception can be demonstrated and also the vehement antagonism which it aroused among more orthodox Hebrews. This led, further, to the conception of Reason as present in the very structure of the physical world and, further again, to a very singular recoil on the part of Ecclesiastes from such a rationalizing of the world and a return by him to a doctrine of the absolute will and control of God. This recoil from a known danger may have put his Book in the Canon.*

*Yet again, the continuing influence of the ideas lying behind the story of Solomon's Dream is very plain. Whenever Hebrews, whether writing in Hebrew or in Greek, thought of Solomon they thought of him as having chosen Reason for his portion and they recognized that Jehovah Himself had approved his choice. Thus Solomon became for them the historical protagonist of Reason and through his authority Reason was fixed in the Hebrew and Jewish mind as desirable and divinely approved. Further, through him the conception of an Eternal Reason—part of, dependent on, or independent of the personality of Jehovah—found a place, in spite of the disapproval of Ecclesiastes, in the inheritance of Israel. Ben Sira and the author of "Wisdom" had to face this conception, use it and limit it as best they could. The author of the Fourth Gospel found another and very different place for it in philosophical theology. It has proved to be one of the great fertilizing ideas in human thinking. Spinoza and the other Hebrew philosophers of the future had so much basis in their racial past for their speculations.*

*In this connection it is not to the point to inquire as to the historicity of the story of Solomon's Dream. Belief in it was plainly a part of the thinking of the Hebrews and our concern is only with how this story affected their philosophical development. Nor is it of much moment to fix dates in that development. There are very few absolutely secure dates for the writings of the Hebrews; we can trace the influence of ideas but can seldom place these precisely in time. Nor is it necessary. It may be of importance to date the reign of a king or the fall of a city, but the ideas of literature exist for themselves, out of space and time. And it was in forms of true creative literature that the original Hebrew philosophers expressed themselves and thus illustrated the essential Platonism of their minds.*

*Need I add finally that I have of purpose refrained from referring to or quoting the enormous literature which has grown up round the Books here considered? My object has been to trace and demonstrate certain ideas in those Books which seem, to me at least, to have been too much neglected. Complete consideration of the history of the interpretation of these Books lay outside of my plan. All the statements as to the occurrences of words and their usages have been elaborately controlled from the concordances.*

*In the last chapter, bringing together the* Laws *of Plato, Ben Sira and Ecclesiastes, I have been compelled to enter on a field strictly alien to the studies of my life. It is right, therefore, to say that I have used for it Dr. Bury's text and translation in the Loeb Classical Library—without it I would have been helpless; also Professor Taylor's translation and introduction and the commentary of Dr. E. B. England.*

*That I have prefixed the Nicene Creed in its commonly accepted form will, I trust, be intelligible. It is the great basal statement of the Christian Faith—incidentally my own—and towards it this whole book points and leads,* per varios casus per tot discrimina rerum. *I prefix it in no spirit of challenge but as a document in the case.*

*Finally, I am greatly indebted to Miss Grace Calverley, B.A., for a careful revision of the whole manuscript. My brother, Norman Macdonald in Glasgow, has had a special care that it should be clear and broadly intelligible to the general educated public.*

—D.B.M.

# CONTENTS

## THE NICENE CREED

*I believe in one God the Father Almighty, Maker of heaven and earth, And of all things visible and invisible:*

*And in one Lord Jesus Christ, the only-begotten Son of God; Begotten of his Father before all worlds, God of God, Light of Light, Very God of very God; Begotten, not made; Being of one substance with the Father; By whom all things were made; Who for us men and for our salvation came down from heaven. And was incarnate by the Holy Ghost of the Virgin Mary, And was made man: and was crucified also for us under Pontius Pilate; He suffered and was buried: And the third day he rose again according to the Scriptures: And ascended into heaven, and sitteth on the right hand of the Father: And he shall come again, with glory, to judge both the quick and the dead; Whose kingdom shall have no end.*

*And I believe in the Holy Ghost, The Lord, and Giver of Life, who proceedeth from the Father and the Son; Who with the Father and the Son together is worshipped and glorified; Who spake by the Prophets: And I believe one Holy Catholic and Apostolic Church: I acknowledge one Baptism for the remission of sins: And I look for the Resurrection of the dead: And the Life of the world to come. Amen.*

# CHAPTER I

# THE ABSOLUTE AS A PERSONALITY

IN THE following pages an attempt will be made to trace in broad outline how philosophical thinking began amongst the Hebrews—if such a fundamental element in life can be said ever to begin; how it developed in their minds; what were its essential characteristics and limitations and what end it reached as a purely Hebrew product. Further, we shall see what happened to Hebrew thought—how strangely and completely it was perverted —when it was taken up into the current of Greek thought and became a very alien strand twisted into the Alexandrine philosophy and theology. The complete contrast between these two stages will show how untouched by Greek philosophy Palestinian Hebrew thinking had been; that is, the thinking that is exhibited in our Old Testament and in such purely Palestinian products as Ecclesiasticus, the Book of Ben Sira. In consequence, an important part of the thesis of the present book will be a demonstration of the originality of Hebrew philosophy as it grew up on its own soil in Palestine, and a disproof of the frequently asserted dependence of Ecclesiastes, Proverbs and Job on Greek influences. This will be shown, on the one hand, by tracing back the ideas of these books to ancient and fundamental Hebrew conceptions and, on another, by showing what actually did happen to Hebrew thinking when it admittedly came under the influence of the Greek thought of Alexandria. Nothing could be more remote from the variously realistic schemes of Ecclesiastes and Proverbs than the vaporous allegories of Philo; his philosophically abstracted deity has nothing in common with the vigorous and directly acting personality of the Jehovah of our Old Testament.

Again, it may be well at the very beginning to state that the basis of this book will not be an array of proof-texts, or even longer quoted passages. A certain limited number of passages will be translated or cited, but the real basis of the book is the broad but assured impression which wide and close and sympathetic reading of the Old Testament has left. It will, therefore, be for the reader of this book to read the Old Testament in the same way and to look beyond incidental and accidental phrases to the spirit breathed by the Hebrews into their literature. If that reading leads to the realization that the spirit of the Hebrews had a profoundly philosophical side, different it may be from Greek philosophy but true philosophy and strongly akin to the mind of Plato, the object of this book will be attained. The spirit of neither a literature nor a philosophy can be conveyed in isolated sentences.

But to return and begin at the beginning: Our inquiry is whether and how far the Hebrew had reached true philosophy. The inquiry is in place because this has been so frequently denied, a denial which shows a limited way of looking at the Old Testament and sheer ignorance of the Hebrew mind. It practically involves the assertion that the Hebrews were so completely dominated by the Revelation from Jehovah that their rational powers were atrophied, so that all that was open to them beyond Revelation was a sacrosanct something called Wisdom, of authoritative divine origin; and that beyond this Wisdom their thinking did not venture to go.

It will be necessary, therefore, to consider the scope for the Hebrews of Revelation and of Reason; how Reason, that is independent thinking, began and how far it went. Revelation, then, meant authoritative utterance from Jehovah, commanding and forbidding, and generally guiding. The essence of it was that it expressed Authority. But we must beware when we use the term Revelation, of thinking of it as certain Revealed Scriptures, that is the Books of our Old Testament. These are simply certain Hebrew writings which contained and conveyed the will of Jehovah and a great many other things besides. In them, along with those other things, is the record of Jehovah's authoritative communications to the Hebrews; or, perhaps better expressed, of the reactions of the Hebrews to those authoritative communications. Those communications took three forms: First there was the Law given in the Mount. This was of different kinds and degrees, simple and elaborate, dealing with different classes of subject, from a law of moral conduct to details for the Tabernacle. It was given by Jehovah Himself and in His own words. Second came continuous guidance of the people through Prophets. The word of Jehovah came to these and they were commissioned to teach and guide the people with the formula, "Thus said Jehovah." The prophets were thus intermediaries, but they taught with authority. There was apparently among them a high and a low doctrine of their office. The high doctrine regarded them as forming part of the Privy Council of Jehovah; they knew His purposes and He kept nothing secret from them. In the low doctrine they were simply channels of communication between Jehovah and men. Then, third, there was the guidance of Jehovah of the individual soul which turned to Him and sought teaching from Him. This way of reaching authoritative truth was open to anyone. The intimacy reached with Jehovah would vary greatly in degree and might practically be the same as that of the prophets. But the essential difference was that this was for personal and individual instruction, while the prophets were commissioned to go out and teach others. We have here, of course, the general mystical doctrine of intercourse with the divine background of life and of immediate intuition of that Divine Reality and instruction by it. The Psalms among the Hebrews were to a great extent the reactions of individuals to this intercourse. But in all these three cases what was communicated came with authority and was to be so received.

The time came for the Jews when the writings which told of these transactions became authority in themselves, but that was later. When that happened, there was gradually built up the gigantic doctrine of the inspiration of Sacred Scripture, factual, verbatim and literatim, from which we have in the last generation freed ourselves. Our necessity now is to realize that though the Hebrews had no such doctrine of Sacred Scripture they had not only a doctrine, but a complete assurance, of an all-dominating and ruling Personality behind life, the Personality of Jehovah. That Personality was no remote Will or Fate—such a Necessity in the background, brooding over everything, as even Plato had in the *Timaeus* (42A, 47E); nor was it any abstract Thinking, removed from relativities and relationships, *bombitans in vacuo,* and needing a Demiurge to connect with the material world, but it was just such a Personality as the Hebrews knew amongst themselves. Nor was it even an ethical Absolute. This Personality could make mistakes and recognize them and correct them. There was thus open to it, on both sides, a possibility and a necessity of mutual understanding with man and of human contacts. Just such friendship and love that existed between individuals of mankind could exist from God to man and from man to God and the same word was used in both cases. The Jehovah of the Hebrews was anthropomorphic, but He was that exactly in the way that made a religious attitude possible and made an abstract, philosophical Absolute exceedingly difficult.

The result of all this is that the fundamental Hebrew conception of a God who reveals Himself to every human soul can still hold for us and can be made the basis of a sound philosophical theology even when the Law revealed in the Mount and the time-limited rhapsodies of the Hebrew prophets have ceased to have weight or meaning for us. The proof-text theology of our parents is utterly gone; systematic theology exists only as, in its ideas, it can be philosophically based; the Hebrew writings are history and not law and their content must justify itself in itself. But the intercourse with the Divine of the Hebrew mystic still remains and is the ultimate Authority for us, an authority that all may test to one degree or another. The specific mystical Vision may be open to few but all may know the Intuition of Duty, "stern daughter of the Voice of God." "One accent of the Holy Ghost the listening world has never lost," and thus is virtue so near to our dust and God so close to man. That the Hebrews knew this utterly and completely and passed it on to the world is their contribution which holds for us still, even when the thunders of Sinai are faint in our ears. This comes from beyond ourselves and is ultimate, unescapable Authority, but it contains, too, within itself depths of philosophical meditation. Relations with an anthropomorphic Personality like Jehovah give far more scope to philosophy than the contemplation in its barrenness of an abstract Absolute. This will be developed hereafter.

But Reason, as one Hebrew asked (Job xxviii, 12, 20), whence does it come and what is the place of Understanding? It is our own thinking from within ourselves and renders our personality and our assured identity. As Jehovah has a personality and has His thoughts which are His own, so is it with each one of us, His creatures. As the Hebrews were so sure of the personality of Jehovah, so they were sure, as cause and consequence, each of his own personality. Beyond their minds there were the facts of life; these facts they observed and tried to understand; and from their understanding they constructed schemes of these facts and of their own place in them. This may sound very modern, but the Hebrews knew all about it. They may not have talked about the percept and the percipient, the knower and the known, and how to bring them together in the unity of knowing, but their speculations went so far that, for some of them, they marred the simplicity of life by finding out too many reckonings (Ecclesiastes vii, 29).

Indeed their respect for the facts of daily life was modern in the highest degree and they recoiled from speculations which were not firmly based on these facts, and required by these facts. Before Occam they felt the absurdity of multiplying beings without cause. The Neoplatonic Chain would have been a baseless and unnecessary unreality to them. Jehovah was their Absolute but He needed no intermediaries to work amongst men. This may be far from the refinements of ontology but it is genuine biological metaphysics. For the facts which they observed and respected were of two kinds. There were the given concrete facts of the physical world and there were the equally given and assured facts of personal experience, their own emotions and ideas. These ideas were real to them, real as the earth on which they trod; they were facts in their consciousness. It is true that they had no such phrase as our "stream of consciousness" and that it would probably have taken a great deal of Hebrew to explain to an ancient Hebrew what we mean by that. But though they had no word or phrase for it, they were in it and knew they were in it—that they were having mental and emotional experiences and reacting to them, each personally in his own way. The poet of Job and the author of Ecclesiastes knew perfectly well that things were befalling their minds one after another, and that they were thinking about these things as they came. The absence of a word in a vocabulary is never evidence for the absence of the idea which the word expresses; thoughts precede their expression in language. Otherwise the ancient Greeks could not have found things "interesting"—a laughable absurdity; for there is no equivalent word in old Greek to our "interest" in that sense. Thus, as we shall see, again and again, the Hebrews, under the dominance of ideas which had come to them, which they had after their fashion tested, and certainly accepted as true, were Platonists rather than Aristotelians; mental facts tended to override the facts of physical experience. An idea, once it had effected a lodgment, had more weight than the plainest external fact.

This comes out very evidently in their relationship to the idea of personality. That idea for the Hebrews overcame everything else. Our "I think therefore I am" and the Muslim "I will therefore I am" was for them "I am therefore I am"—an expression of their egocentric subjectivity. Personality is its own proof and the proof of its own right of existence. In consequence the Hebrew was a matured form of the child who places himself in existence quite simply with, "This is Me." Quite possibly we have here a desert inheritance, for there can be no question of the stark, even ferocious, individualism of the desert Arabs still. Personalities, then, were the primary facts in life and their Absolute presented itself to them as a supreme Personality, a personality as real and assured as any of their own. This is a philosophical statement of the notion of the relation of Jehovah to Israel, but it is not in the least historical. It may put that relation in our terms of thinking, but for the Hebrews it is plain that Jehovah was simply a fact of experience, as each one of themselves was to every other, only He was a stupendous and overwhelming fact. As to the origin of the fact we have no clue. Its origin did not lie in their subjective individualism, for the desert Arabs developed no such figure and were indeed singularly indifferent to any such divine element behind their lives. Nor was it a result of philosophical deduction. Whenever and wherever we meet the Hebrews we meet, as though one of themselves, this figure of Jehovah. They knew He was not one of themselves and had vague, half-suppressed, mythological ideas on what He was, but He was as immediate to them, and now to us, as though He were one of themselves.

To bring this out more clearly let us look at the contrasting situation among the Greeks. Theologically the Greeks were in an entirely different position. When they looked at the facts of life and tried to work back through them to a unified view of the world and their own place in it, to a philosophical grasp, that is, of the world in the broadest sense, and still more, when they tried to reach a religious attitude possible for a thinking man, their religious inheritance was a positive handicap. They were compelled tacitly to abandon it. If any figure in it was to be retained as a religious ultimate, that could be done only by stripping from that figure all the elements which made up its personality and reducing it to a blank Absolute. So we have the puzzle of the Zeus of Plato, an abstraction which he calls God but which certainly can have excited in him no emotional attitude. He may call him "the begetting Father" as an attempted escape from the philosophical mystery of creation in time, but all his readers knew that this was only a surviving fragment of myth and contributed nothing of personality to his "God." Marcus Aurelius, long after and following other suggestions, might represent the Kingdom of Heaven as the "City of Zeus" and there might grow up, under still other influences, a picture of Zeus, the Saviour. But for Plato and the thinking men of his time the desire was rather to get away from the personal characteristics of the Zeus that they knew. All this is in the sharpest contrast to the religious attitude, for example, of David and Amos to Jehovah. David in the Eighteenth Psalm is certainly, for our modern evangelical emotion, quite unregenerate but his intimacy with Jehovah is warm, deep and real and his trust in Jehovah is complete. Amos, on his part, for all the austere magnificence of his Jehovah, is so intimate with Him that he gives the impression of carrying Jehovah in his pocket. He, Amos, knows all about Jehovah, is in His secrets and can turn Him to his own purpose. Such an attitude in both cases was possible because Jehovah was a person and fitted like a person into the life of the Israelites. On one side they need make no allowances or apologies for Him or for His ways with men, and on another, they had solved the problem of domesticating the Absolute. No philosophical categories came between them and the object of their worship.

What, then, was the inheritance of the Greeks which made a religious attitude so difficult for their thinkers and which drove them to unemotional philosophies? They had two religious inheritances, one literary and esthetic and the other popular and primitive. Those two had certainly their points of contact, each with the other, and it is only in recent years that the second, and its importance, have become in any way separate and clear to us. The first we know from Homer and Hesiod and the Greek poets generally; it tells of the genealogies of the gods, of Zeus and his court on Olympus, of the heavenly mythology as a whole. Because of this, the poems of Homer have been called the Bible of the Greeks and there is a certain aptness in the name. Greek youth was brought up upon them as we used to be on the Bible. But for Greek thinkers this seems to have been a necessary evil. They were perfectly aware of the more than dubious morals of these Olympians and of the multitudinous scandals of their lives. The stories about them had entered into the very fiber of Greek thinking and all education was built upon them. But how corrupting were the examples and incitements in them! Our nursery tales have been denounced as an evil influence on childhood, but what if Jack the Giant-killer and his like were also held up as objects of religious worship? And the morals of the Greek gods were much less estimable than those of Jack. It is therefore quite intelligible that Greek moralists and philosophers should keep as far as possible from such unclean tales. For these were not simply primitively ferocious as that of Jack and his like but they were unclean as well. There is a significant fragment of an ode which Pindar was commissioned to write on the presentation of a bevy of slave-girls to the shrine of Aphrodite for the purposes of her rites. But Pindar plainly did not like his task and shows the workings of a decent conscience against it. So it may be said quite roundly that the Olympians from Zeus downwards were a grievous handicap to the religious striving of Greece. Zeus, for religious purposes, stands in ludicrous contrast to Jehovah.

The other religious inheritance was that connected with the primitive deities of the soil. This showed itself in rites of fertility-worship and in its most spiritual form developed into the Mysteries. So it may be said that the Mysteries carried the real religious life of the classical world; in them the Greeks were brought into contact with the fundamental verities, the necessities and the pathos of life. This was done in a sacramental fashion by symbols and pictures which suggested ever widening thoughts. Dramas of life and death were put before the initiates and they were guided in underworld journeys. So the attempt was made to develop the very simple worship of fertility and of the reproductive processes into allegories of the meaning of life. But this form of religion, too, suffered under grievous handicaps. It was secret and esoteric. The open side consisted of frankly naturalistic mythological stories and the secret side, which undoubtedly attracted thinking and devout men, suffered by its origin from such primitive conceptions. Both sides, whatever their associations with the ever renewed life of the world, were dull and hopeless. It was an underworld religion, and under the spell of inexorable Hades. It was liable also to perversion into such rites of the imprecation of evil as we know as the Black Mass.

The comparison with the Hebrew Sheol lies here very near. But the religious-minded Hebrews knew very well that the conception of Sheol belonged to heathen Semitism and had no religious value, and they tried to get rid of it as much as possible. Their hope was in the dominating personality of Jehovah and in the possibility of abiding and intimate contact with Him. Sheol and Abaddon lie open before Him and how much more the hearts of the Sons of human kind (Proverbs xv, 11). So here again the Hebrew had the religious advantage of the relation of every man to an individual like himself.

But these two Greek inheritances, also, were quite irreconcilable with Greek science, whether Aristotelian or Platonic. This meant that the conflict of religion and science as we know it had already for the Greeks begun. But the Hebrews never had a conflict of religion and science. The laws governing the nature of their world were the thoughts of Jehovah and a conflict might as easily be imagined between the shadowy Zeus of Plato and the laws of the universe as laid down in the *Timaeus*. The Hebrews had their problem about Jehovah but it was an entirely different problem. He was for them a person, their ultimate, and in final control. A person was behind life for them and not simply a material universe involving a bundle of mythological ideas. *Their Absolute was a Person.* How could the Absolute be a person? For our philosophy it could only be by shedding all limitations and so ceasing to be an individual. But the Hebrew took the great leap of the mystic and held both the absoluteness and the personality of

Jehovah. It is instructive in this connection to observe how Philo, bent on turning Jehovah into a philosophical Absolute, an abstract pure being, had to get rid, by allegorical interpretations, of all the characteristics of the Jehovah of the Old Testament. Neither David nor Amos nor any Hebrew would ever have recognized the vapid abstraction with which Philo comes out as the Jehovah they had known. This is an extreme case but actual and very suggestive. Similarly Plato had to ignore the characteristics of the Zeus of the poets and mythologists and retain only the name. Philo's method of escape by allegory, with all its unrealities, Plato probably knew better than to attempt; so he simply ignored the accepted characteristics of Zeus. It was left for the Neoplatonists to follow in the path of Philo and to turn the stories about the Olympians into myths, theological, physical, psychical. This is brought out very plainly in the little creed, or almost catechism, of Sallustius, the close friend of the Emperor Julian, which is translated by Professor Gilbert Murray as an appendix to his *Four Stages of Greek Religion.*

But the Hebrews, who retained Jehovah as a person with all the characteristics which He shows in the Old Testament and exhibited to them in life, had still their problem. What was His character when analyzed? Was He moral, as men judge morals? Was He considerate of man or indifferent to man? Was He—and this cuts even deeper—really intelligible to man? And to go still further: This world of His, was it a rational world as men understand Reason? Science for the Hebrews meant knowledge of the world as He had made it and was administering it; the laws of the world were His thoughts and will, and of necessity led back to Him. These thoughts formed a system and hung together. But could men grasp that system; could they think God's thoughts after Him? Man had a certain Reason as his guide in life but was it the same as Jehovah's Reason by which He guided the universe? Men had observed the facts of life and also that there were certain intellectual and moral elements in themselves. Were these the same in Jehovah? If they were, what did that mean as to the origin of man and as to Jehovah's purpose for man? Was man just a part of the world or was he the crown of the world and the reason for its existence? In all that lay abundant questions and possibilities of conflict. But they were psychological questions and not physical; the Hebrews were philosophers and not physicists. Their possible conflict was not of science and religion but of God and man. For the personality of Jehovah was being scrutinized, weighed and judged by man. So their philosophy in the ultimate analysis, while always remaining theistic, might be irreligious in several different degrees and ways. That is its uniqueness and interest; and in all its attitudes it was a true philosophy.

# CHAPTER II

# A PHILOSOPHY OF BECOMING

THE last chapter consisted of certain preliminary considerations to which we shall cast back again and again. The philosophical Absolute of the Hebrews was, as we have seen, the Personality of Jehovah. But, while all the Hebrews accepted this, they had also reached and held along with it certain other definite philosophical positions. Four of these it may be well to work out even at this point, as they lie behind what may be called the Hebrew conscious philosophical thinking. They are: (i) the existence of conscience and consciousness; (ii) that all things are in flux and becoming; (iii) that Life is an essential reality; (iv) that evil is stupidity.

First, then, they recognized that man had a moral sense of his own and that he could freely exercise that moral sense. In spite of the absolute personality behind life, man possessed what we call free will. This is shown by the fact that he could thwart and irritate Jehovah. For that Jehovah could punish him; but man was no automaton; he was as free as Jehovah Himself. This was recognized so absolutely that it was taken for granted. We find reflections upon it but no philosophical explanation of it or attempt to make it agree with Jehovah's unlimited control of the world. By it man was in mind and spirit outside of that control. That was a fundamental fact, and the farthest any Hebrew got was to recognize that it made the difference between man and what we call the lower animals. We have reached a word for this independent moral sense and we call it "conscience"; the Hebrew had no word and had to use the phrase "knowing good and evil." (Genesis ii, 9-17.) Or rather, a philosopher finding no word for it had to apply that descriptive phrase, used already in the language for different purposes. Thus in 2 Samuel xix, 35, "Can I know (distinguish) between good and evil?" Here it is not ethical; compare, too, Deuteronomy i, 39. Other Hebrews got along without it, just as in French to this day *conscience* means both our "consciousness" and our "conscience" and even the self-conscious Greeks used συνείδησις and its cognates for both the psychological and the ethical conceptions. But to bring home how the ordinary, not philosophical-minded, Hebrew expressed "conscience" for himself, let the English reader of the Old Testament consider a word that is used multitudinously in his version, the word "heart." It is in all but a very few cases the literal rendering of one Hebrew word in two closely similar forms. But it will be evident to the most careless reader that, as often as not, the context requires some phase or other of the idea "mind." And the fact is that this Hebrew word was the ordinary Hebrew word for "mind." The Greek translators of the Septuagint knew this perfectly well and they rendered it by a number of Greek words, διάνοια, νοῦς, ὁμόνοια, συνίημι, φρόνησις, ψυχή, ἐπιθυμία, all suggesting "mind," besides the literal καρδία, "heart." And in certain cases it is quite plain that the Hebrew word meant exactly our "conscience." Thus in Job xxvii, 6, "My heart (conscience) does not reproach me since my earliest days." 1 Samuel xxiv, 6, "And it happened thereafter that David's heart (conscience) smote him"; 1 Samuel xxv, 31, "And this shall not be to thee a stumbling-block of heart (conscience)," i.e. a cause of future remorse. In the translation of the New Testament into Hebrew by Franz Delitzsch, a master of Hebrew usage, the Greek word for "conscience" συνείδησις is most frequently rendered by this Hebrew word for "heart." "To be conscious" and "consciousness" are more difficult and abstract, but they are involved in all operations of the mind even though not explicitly named. In at least one passage this Hebrew word "heart" seems used to suggest a state of consciousness. In Song of Songs v, 2, "I am sleeping but my heart (consciousness) is waking." In this context it is to be remembered that the Hebrew "heart" was not, as with us, the seat of love. This is only one illustration of how behind a Hebrew concrete term there may lie quite a subtle idea. Another Hebrew word had to bear a similar weight of varying usage. It is the common verb "to know" and the reader of our English versions should stop at each case and consider what is implied in the context. He will find that that Hebrew verb is always emphatic and has often in it the meaning "to know intimately," "to be on intimate, personal, terms with. . . ." Thus "to know" is used regularly as a decent expression for knowing sexually and, at another extreme, for Jehovah's unique personal relation to Israel, "With you only have I been on intimate personal terms. . . ." (Amos iii, 2.) In consequence, it is used to express our conception "to be consciously aware, realize" and thus simply "to be conscious." This is very plain in Proverbs vii, 23, "and he does not know (is not conscious, does not realize) that it is for his life," and in Joshua xxiii, 14, "and ye know (are fully conscious) in all your mind and in all your soul that. . . ." This last comes very close to an expression of self-consciousness.

But for the philosopher of Genesis the idea had become explicit and he applied a phrase which exactly expressed it. His Hebrew phrase meant that man knew for himself the categories Good and Bad and could distinguish cases by the operation of his own mind. This is the explicit point of the third chapter of Genesis and is implicit throughout the Old Testament. We find everywhere the working of man's reason as a moral guide in life, and as clearly opposed to dependence on the specific commands of Jehovah. The story in Genesis is evidently a philosophical reflection on the observed fact that man has a moral sense. It is somewhat obscured, of course, by being expressed through the means of a quite different folklore tale, but the facts of the observation and reflection are plain enough. When was the reflection made or, rather, as the reflection must be very old, when was it put into this form and expressed in this way? As to that we have no clue. The author of Ecclesiastes knew Genesis well, but we can get no further. Certain questions and surmises remain. Folklore knows many Trees of Life and the like, but this Tree of Knowing Good and Evil seems to be unique and it enters into no Babylonian legend. It may easily be an addition of the philosopher who used the legend of the origin of woman for his own purposes. It is singular also that man's attaining this independent moral sense and becoming a self-determining moral being should have taken place against the will of Jehovah. Is this simply part of the awkwardness of using primitive myths as vehicles of philosophical teachings, or did the philosopher appreciate the sardonic point involved? Again we cannot tell, but it is noteworthy that, while the evil tendencies in man's nature are always referred to the unclean materials—dust from the soil—

out of which he was made, the argument that man's moral sense must be part of his created nature and therefore came from God is never used. Both the Poet of Job and Ecclesiastes criticize God freely for the moral defects in His government of the world. They thus apply to God a canon of right and wrong which they have in themselves. But they never consider, nor do Job's Friends urge it against him, that if this canon belongs to their created nature God, too, their creator, must possess it. Did Ecclesiastes and the Poet of Job regard it, as in the Genesis story, as an addition to man's created nature and indeed, acquired against the will of God? But that would be very difficult to maintain, for throughout the whole Old Testament man's power of moral choice and freedom of will are taken for granted. It is taken for granted also that in spite of man's knowledge of good and evil he has a specific tendency to go wrong. How far the moral defeatism of the Prophets is responsible for this may be a further question. But that the Hebrews recognized the fact of conscience stands fast and that, so far, man was outside of the control of Jehovah. Whatever the Hebrews were, they were not Calvinists of any type. Jehovah might be the ultimate ruler and a dominating personality but men were personalities also and had their fate in their own hands. There are even signs, as in the Speeches of the Lord in Job, that man, for some Hebrews, was a disturbing element in nature, and that the natural world could get along very well without man. It had a life of its own and Jehovah enjoyed looking on, upon that life. But man tried to dominate in nature; to use nature for his own ends; and neither nature nor Jehovah liked that. So hostility arises between man and the creatures of the non-human world, and Jehovah is on the side of the beasts. This is only one phase of the working of this conception of human personality in the Hebrew mind and there were many others. Here, as everywhere in the Old Testament writings, we must beware of thinking that the Hebrews had one clear-cut scheme of life.

A second position which the Hebrews had reached and which they held with unanimity is probably most of all responsible for their reputation as an unphilosophically minded people. Philosophy admittedly must be metaphysical, that is it must be concerned with what lies behind and beyond the physical world. In that "beyond" it may seek an explanation of the physical world but it must reach beyond that world. But for metaphysics a very common quasi-synonym is ontology and ontology means strictly the science of Being. In consequence it has become a fixed idea that a basal element in any philosophy must be the notion of Being and that any thinking which does not recognize the notion of Being cannot be a philosophy. It does not seem to matter that some Greek philosophers made great play of the distinction of Being and Becoming and even held that Being was a non-existent and meaningless, even useless and misleading abstraction. For Heracleitus of Ephesus all things were Becoming and could never be caught in a state of Being. All things are flowing, he held, and you cannot step into the same stream twice. You cannot say of the stream that it "is," for it is in constant change. The notion of Being is static and can never apply to this world of ours, animate or inanimate. Least of all can it apply to the constantly flowing stream of our thoughts. The modern phrase of a "stream of consciousness," he would have said, was a supreme illustration that the true ultimate reality was Becoming.

With this conception of the ultimate reality the Hebrews would have been in entire agreement. Their ultimate reality was the personality of Jehovah and a personality cannot be static. From the beginning of their thinking history they were Heracleitans and had no question that all things were flowing, changing, becoming. *The concept Being did not exist for them.* This is fundamental even to their language. In classical Hebrew, just as in classical Arabic, there is no verb "to be," either as an expression of the logical copula or of the idea of existence. The logical copula, as in "Every *A* is *B*," is left unexpressed, except syntactically, in both Hebrew and Arabic, and Hebrew has no way of expressing simple existence, except syntactically. In Arabic philosophical writing the verb "to find" has been called into service to express existence. "It exists" is literally "it is found" and "an entity, an existent thing" is "a thing found." And this, in the case of the Hebrews, is not a simple inadequacy of their language but renders the Hebrew attitude towards life and the universe and their Absolute. They had no need of Being, for to their minds everything was Becoming. Everything for them was in perpetual change, in process of becoming and passing. This is obscured for us often in our English versions by the fact that the English *Be* can really mean *Become*. "Let there be light" is good English for "Let Light come into existence," as the Hebrew means; and so again and again. And, above all, this holds explicitly of Jehovah himself. His existence did not lie in any eternal static Being as did that of Plato's God in the *Timaeus*. Zeus for Plato had Being, pure existence, in an eternal, changeless world. He was not in Time. This world of ours is in Time and is a world of change and Becoming. Jehovah, too, Absolute and Ultimate as he was, was in Time and in Becoming and in perpetual change, because in constant adaptation to new situations. He was a dynamic Personality, as opposed to a static and needed no intermediary for contact with a world of change and differences. It is a singular illustration of the completeness with which a fixed idea can obscure facts that Philo and the Alexandrine Jews in general, being soaked in Greek ontology, were blind to the true nature of their own Jehovah and turned Him into an onto-logical abstract Being, stripped of His characteristics and separate from His world. This compelled them to develop the Word of Jehovah into a personified Demiurge as a link with the world. Unhappily Philo used the Greek term Logos in the sense Word, for this being—though he also used the same word in the sense, "reason"—and thus confused the conception in the Christian Church of the meaning of the Logos in the Prologue to the Fourth Gospel. But this anticipates. To return: Are we, then, to deny to the Hebrews a philosophy because they did not invent a notion and a word for which there was no corresponding reality in their world or behind their world?

But to what extent did the Hebrews consciously recognize the notion of Becoming as fundamental to their world? It is naïvely present in the simplicity with which their minds accepted the fact that Jehovah might change His mind, might even recognize that some action on His part had been a mistake. Our versions render this commonly that God "repented him" of this or that, even of the creation of man in the earth. Not so naïvely but with deep moral insight David recognized that the Jehovah whom he knew so well adjusted Himself to the different qualities and characteristics of the men whom He had Himself created. They, too, were personalities, and so differing, and His treatment of each of them differed. That David exactly describes:

> With a friendly man Thou showest Thyself friendly; with a blameless man Thou showest Thyself blameless; with a sincere man Thou showest Thyself sincere; but with a crook Thou showest Thyself harshly hard. For it is Thou a lowly folk that savest, but lofty eyes Thou bringest low. (Psalm xviii, 25-27.)

The fact that Jehovah becomes all things to all men could not be put more clearly. They are personalities who have become what they have become by their own free working, but Jehovah meets them in all their becomings.

This characteristic of Jehovah is expressed in more abstract and philosophical form in two passages in Exodus. Generally the philosopher-artist who created for us our Genesis seems to have lifted his hand when he came to the Book of Exodus which undoubtedly lay before him as did the proto-Genesis. Apparently he despaired of bringing order into that chaos. But at two points where Jehovah describes Himself and gives Himself a Name the philosopher felt compelled to explain it in the same fashion that he had used before with the folklore stories in early Genesis. In Exodus iii, 13-15 we read:

> "See, I am going to the Sons of Israel and I shall say to them, 'The God of your fathers hath sent me to you.' Then they will say to me, 'What is His name?' What shall I say to them?" (14) And God said to Moses "I become (*Ehyé*) what I become." And He said [further], "Thus shalt thou say to the Sons of Israel, 'I become' (*Ehyé*) has sent me to you." (15) And God said again to Moses "Thus shalt thou say to the Sons of Israel 'Jehovah [probably pronounced Yahwé], the God of your fathers, the God of Abraham, the God of Isaac and the God of Jacob hath sent me to you. This is my name forever and this is my memory to generation of generation.'"

In this passage Moses is given a proper name for this God of their ancestors who has appeared to him and sent him to the Sons of Israel. That proper name which in English has become Jehovah, was probably pronounced Yahwé but we have no certainty as to its original meaning or derivation. The philosopher, however, sees here a possibility of bringing out clearly the character of the personality of Jehovah as opposed to some archaic name the meaning of which apparently was lost. Or he may only be using one of those puns which Hebrew rhetoric loved so well and allowed in all contexts. Elsewhere in Exodus, as vi, 2, 3, the name is given as Jehovah (Yahwé) and that, in some form or other, e.g. Yah, Yahu, was certainly the traditional name of God among the Hebrews. But in the passage quoted above from chapter iii it is plain that its meaning was either unknown or so obscure that the philosopher found it possible to play upon it in this way and to make this insertion in the text of Exodus in order to bring out clearly his conception of God's basal character. This means that iii, 14 is his insertion and that the original answer to the question of Moses in verse 13 is in verse 15. The text certainly reads much more smoothly without verse 14. But most unhappily a perversion of the meaning of verse 14 began with the Greek version and has continued ever since. The Greek-speaking Jew in Egypt translated the important verb here with the Greek verb to Be instead of to Become. They rendered here, "I am the one who is" ('Εγώ εἰμι ὁ ὤν), and "The one who is (ὁ ὤν) has sent me to you." The proper name Jehovah (however it was written in their Hebrew text) they rendered uniformly "The Lord" (ὁ κύριος). The point of the Hebrew could not be more completely concealed; a purely ontological conception has been substituted for an assertion of constant change. Thus we have in the text and margin of our English Revised Version four different translations all equally impossible. And similarly all speculations in the Christian Church, from the Greek Fathers down, on the meaning of this passage and of this statement as to the name of God have been vitiated by following the Greek translation instead of going back to the Hebrew itself. It is significant that Driver in his commentary on Exodus, following Robertson Smith and A. B. Davidson, sees this point quite clearly but hesitates to state a clean-cut conclusion. (*Exodus* in *The Cambridge Bible*, pp. 23 and 40.)

In Exodus xxxiii there is apparently a similar insertion and with the same object to bring out the broad adaptability of the character of Jehovah. It is in that very naïve scene where Moses is not allowed to see the face of Jehovah but only His back. In verse 18 Moses says, "Please to show me thy glory." "Glory" is used here, as sometimes in emphatic, exalted language, in the sense of "self," "personality." In verse 19 Jehovah replies, "I will make all my goodness pass before thee, and I will make proclamation using the name of Jehovah before thee, and I will be gracious unto whom I will be gracious and I will show compassion unto whom I shall show compassion." (20) And He said, "Thou canst not see my face for mankind cannot see me and live." Here verse 19 contains a statement of that same adaptability to men on the part of Jehovah and it is coupled with a proclamation of His name Jehovah. If the name given were not Jehovah but "I become" (*Ehyé*) the parallel would be complete. But, again, there can be no question that verse 19 breaks the context between verses 18 and 20. The whole point in these two passages, then, is a statement by Jehovah. "I show myself under many aspects, becoming this and that. I do this to meet you in your needs and you must take me as you find me." Jehovah was the metaphysic of the Hebrews and their metaphysic was not of Being but Becoming.

A third position of the Hebrews stands in essential connection with this second. With growing clearness of perception they faced the question, Why do we keep on living and acting? Their answer, in a word, is that there is in the world a mysterious and ultimate reality called Life. The Hebrew writings are full of phrases bringing this out as an essential fact of existence. Its implications only gradually become plain, but the processes of constant change which make up the existence of the world and of man in it and of God Himself are expressions of this reality, Life. The emphasis on it is strong all through the philosophizing of the Book of Genesis and it is hard to believe that it is not intentionally so. Certainly the positions of Genesis culminate in a brilliant transformation in the Book of Ecclesiastes, and in that book there is full recognition of the fact, if also mystery, of the *élan vital* which keeps us going on. In Genesis man is a compound of dust and life and the life is a living wind which God blew into man and so man became, in the literal Hebrew, "a living desire" (Genesis ii, 7). There was implanted in man something which transformed him from a mere earthen image to a creature that lived and desired. And "desire" in essence is simply desire to continue the self and to keep going on. For it is to be observed that the word in the

Old Testament which is so frequently and misleadingly translated "soul" means fundamentally that phase of the personality which possesses appetites and in old-fashioned psychology might have been called the appetitive soul. That, then, was brought under "life" by the Hebrews and was fundamental to man. It was given to him directly by God. In Genesis vi, 3 it is called "spirit," another word of manifold application, for in Genesis vii, 22 "wind of living spirit" is said to be "in the nostrils" of all the living creatures on the earth which died in the Flood. Life, then, is emphasized as the basal thing in the world beyond the material substance. It is used of plants (Psalm lviii, 10) and even of the return of the year in spring (Genesis xviii, 10, 11; 2 Kings iv, 16, 17). And life means the solidarity of the human race. In Genesis iii, 20 Man gives to his wife the name Hawwá and it is explained that he did so rightly "for she became the mother of all living." This name evidently belonged to the folklore tale and what it meant originally is not clear, but in the explanation it is taken as meaning, or suggesting, *Living*. And this middle earth of ours on which we live is "the land of the living." (Ezekiel xxvi, 20; xxxii, 23, 25, 26, 27, 32) as opposed to the places of the dead, however their existence was conceived, literally "the land of the under-places." Life is conceived as the supreme characteristic and difference of the human race in its existence here on the surface of the earth, "under the sun" as Ecclesiastes reiterates. And life is also a characteristic of Jehovah Himself from the earliest folklore ideas and semi-mythological conceptions. In the story of Hagar (Genesis xvi, 13), "And she called the name of Jehovah who was speaking to her, 'Thou art a God of seeing,' for she had said, 'Have I even here seen after my seer?' Therefore people called the well, *A Well of the Living One, my seer*." (cf. Genesis xxiv, 62; xxv, 11.) "Seen after my seer" is the only possible translation of the present Hebrew text but the meaning is very obscure and the text is probably corrupt. This story and the name of the well must go very far back into ancient legend and embody primitive ideas but their present importance is to emphasize that for the earliest Hebrews in their stories Jehovah was emphatically alive and a presence that saw and took thought for suffering men. There is a curious allusion to this story in the Greek version of Numbers xiv, 21, where

there is the addition "and Living is my name." Similarly the Life
of Jehovah is sworn by again and again; "As Jehovah lives" is
a normal formula. The same holds of men; "As the King lives,"
and the like is common usage. At least twelve times we find the
phrase "the living God." This may be in contrast to the gods of
heathen which are only dead images, but the phrase apparently
goes far back before the iconoclastic fervors of the later prophets
(Hosea vii, 10). For man's yearning back to "the living God" see
Psalms xlii, 2; lxxxiv, 2. God lives and men live and they draw
their life from Him directly, as we have seen. This makes the
difference between them—along with, indeed, all animate things
—and the lifeless material of their bodies. There is nothing
spiritual about this in the exalted sense of the spirit; it is simply
plain life. Nor did it mean for the Hebrew spiritual continuation
beyond our physical death. The biological phenomenon of life, to
speak technically, was common to and united God and men, but
ceased for men with their deaths in the world. And so God was
the God of the living and not of the dead. This is the position over-
whelmingly throughout the Old Testament. Among the later Hebrews we get a few scattered allusions, mainly by way of rejection,
to a doctrine of what we could call spiritual immortality. It is
unnecessary to reiterate here what has already been given on this
subject in *The Hebrew Literary Genius* (Chapters v, ix, xi), dealing with the doctrine of Genesis and Ecclesiastes, the Laments of
David and the place of the Weird in Hebrew thought. Physical
life, then, as we would call it, in God and man was an essential
and fundamental fact for the Hebrews. In the early chapters of
Genesis its importance is beaten in by allusion after allusion but
there is no systematic, what we might call philosophical, statement
upon it. That the world could not exist without it is implied but
never said. But when we reach Ecclesiastes, the Book that uses,
continues and develops Genesis so strangely, we find an explicit
doctrine on the subject. The Book is full of life, but it is life here in
this world, under the sun, and other life there is none. But it is in
men as a present fact and it gives them a zest in life, a desire to go
on living, however hard, abhorrent and hopeless the facts of life
may be. Ecclesiastes is perfectly sure of this inner drive to go on
living and doing; it is a fundamental fact for him in his existence.

And for him it is a primary duty to obey this impulse, a duty which he owes to Life itself. He feels very sure that he owes no duty to God. God is the ultimate Absolute behind everything and an Absolute which must not be irritated; that would mean anger and destruction. But this strange thing Life is different. It is as though Ecclesiastes had made it for himself, almost turned it into a person—personalities were ever the most real things for all Hebrews —and now must help it to carry on and be himself part of it in so carrying on. Such Life had been a reality for the Hebrews from the beginning; now Ecclesiastes looks at it and thinks about it consciously. Only once does he find a word for this mysterious quality in him and in all men which makes them carry on. In one of the most hopeless sections of his book (iv, 1-6) in which he laboriously explains how the haps of life fall upon all alike, indifferent whether they strike the good or the bad, and how death and nothingness wait for all, and how in consequence the minds of men are full of evil and madness, he suddenly throws in "But for whoever is [still] one with all the living there is hope; for to a living dog it is better than to a dead lion." To be alive, therefore, is everything. Life brings with it a trust, blind it may be; accept it and follow its Gleam. Live and exhaust the possibilities of life. And so there comes in verses 7 *ff.* one of the most direct exhortations to the enjoyment of life in the fullest sense, an enjoyment quickened and sharpened by the fact of the inevitable death that lies beyond. But what is this mysterious "hope" or "trust" inherent in anyone who is alive? The exact word occurs elsewhere only in 2 Kings xviii, 19, which is parallel to Isaiah xxxv, 4, and this is Ecclesiastes' only use of it. Nor does the root ever occur in Ecclesiastes although it is very common elsewhere in the sense to feel trust, confidence, security in something or some one, whether rightly or wrongly, wisely or foolishly. It is used, too, of a general trustful attitude. Apparently this means that Ecclesiastes recognized that one of the components of healthy life was a trustful, hopeful feeling towards the future, even though such hopefulness were intellectually and experientially unjustifiable and foolish. This is one of his keenest psychological observations. Hope springs eternal in the human breast, and when hope is gone life is surely ebbing away. We go on in courage through our lives just because we do not know the future. If we knew the future, even a future mixed with much good, we would not have the courage to face it. This is, perhaps, the deepest and most essential point of mystery in living and this Hebrew Ecclesiastes puts his discerning finger upon it. The Hebrews, just because of the importance which they ascribed to personality, were masters of the science and art of living. They watched its currents flow in themselves and in others; they saw the thing Life behind the constant and multitudinous changes of living; and here Ecclesiastes lifts out of life its deepest and most abiding element. How far this was present consciously in the re-iteration upon life of the philosopher of the Book of Genesis is a very difficult problem. He certainly did not tell all he thought and believed; that was not his object in reworking those primitive stories with which he dealt. But Ecclesiastes in his Book did thoroughly clear his soul and free his mind, for that was his object. And we cannot be blind to the close connection between the two books. We may even suspect that behind them there lay a School, for Ecclesiastes reads often like a psychological commentary on Genesis. But when or through what ages that School flourished is another question. A wide gap there must have been for Ecclesiastes is undoubtedly very late and Genesis equally certainly is written in pure, classical Hebrew. It may be that Ecclesiastes took up the threads of thinking spun long before by the unknown philosopher, for assuredly the beginnings of the threads are there in Genesis.

Another problem lies in the New Testament statement "God is not the God of the dead, but of the living." It is found with slight variants as a saying of Christ in the three Synoptic Gospels (Matthew xxii, 32; Mark xii, 27; Luke xx, 38), but never in so many words in the Old Testament as we have it. Luke has the addition, "for all live unto him," i.e. God, which links the saying of Christ with the frequent Pauline doctrine of life towards God, in and through Christ, and still more with Hebrews ix, 14, "to serve the living God," and with I Peter iv, 2 as to living the rest of our time, "to the will of God." The application by Christ Himself in all the three Gospel passages is that, as God is the God of Abraham, Isaac and Jacob, these must still be alive. But all this is very remote from the Old Testament teaching as to the living God. For in the Old Testament, as we have seen, while Jehovah is emphatically living, His relations are only with men here in this world, men who are alive in the physical sense. Neither David nor Amos, for example, ever thought of God as having relations to the dead, however they may have pictured to themselves the state of the dead. So for almost all the Hebrews throughout Old Testament times that saying could have meant only an assertion that Jehovah was not the God of the dead—that the dead had no God at all. But as applied by Christ it means that the physically dead are still alive, for God is still their God and His life is their life. In the later Christian doctrine, through Christ they live to serve God. This application of the saying is of interest here only as showing how complete a change came between the development of thinking in the Old Testament and the Jewish thought of the time of Christ. A new world had arisen and the only element in it that carried on the old Hebrew doctrine was the sect of the Sadducees who said that there was no resurrection, neither angel nor spirit (Matthew xxii, 23; Mark xii, 18; Luke xx, 27; Acts xxiii, 8). This was a legitimate development of the old Hebrew position, and Amos, for example, was a Sadducee before Sadoc, for he reduced the whole world of spirits to Jehovah Himself alone and had no doctrine of spiritual continuance after death.

A fourth philosophical position of the Hebrews was their conception of the nature of evil in man. For the Hebrew psychologist the source of evil in individual man was essentially stupidity. A bad man was a fool of one kind or another, and they had a wide vocabulary to describe fools. This was the result of their observation of men in the world as they acted and spoke. And this position was held not simply by the pragmatic moralist of the Book of Proverbs who held that Jehovah was good and was in complete control of the world; therefore be good and you will be prosperous. It was held also by Ecclesiastes who had no illusions as to the goodness of Jehovah. For him the sinner was a blunderer, always putting his foot in it, and not a rational man, and the ultimate morality was not to be a fool. The equations that badness is stupidity and that stupidity is badness belong to the very fiber of Hebrew thinking. But we must carefully distinguish this personal evil from the impersonal evil of suffering and misfortune. The problem, that is, of unmerited suffering with which the whole

Book of Job wrestles, stands by itself. It leads out to questions of cosmic evil, of the wickedness in the heavenly places of which St. Paul speaks (Ephesians vi, 10) and which affects men, but does not spring from men. Is the world in its essential nature and structure indifferent to good and evil or even specifically evil? For the Hebrew that question came to be a question as to the character of Jehovah Himself. Is man, then, driven to use his wits to conform to the structure of the world or to evade it as far as possible? Again, here, morality is a question of intelligence. Morality, that is, as related to God and His rule of the world. But Hebrew thinkers, as we have seen already, had reached an innate morality of their own, a moral imperative unrelated for them to the working and will of God. They knew good and evil in an absolute sense, a sense which led them beyond their normal Absolute, Jehovah. Job is facing and outfacing Jehovah in the sense in which Prometheus faced Zeus. And it was observation and dialectic which brought these Hebrews to this suicidal pass. Thus the drift of all Hebrew thinking, as thinking, was to link up morals and intelligence.

From this the doctrine of the prophets was a current apart. They set themselves against this observing, critical, reflecting attitude of the people and tried to create a moral category which was linked with the character of Jehovah. Their basis was in essence the mystical revelation and the religious attitude produced by dependence on it. They thought of Jehovah as did the homely moralist in Proverbs, but with a deeper emotional fervor of adoring love. They were perfectly sure; and on this perfect sureness they built up their system. In the building up they used all the resources of argument, rhetoric and emotion, but behind it all was the leap of the mystic. Theirs was thus strictly a nonrational system although it used, as mysticism always does, the methods of reason to work out and bring to bear its superrationally learned laws. In doing this they took terms and epithets and gave to them new and quite different meanings. One of the most significant of these changes was made on a certain very frequent Hebrew word *hôté'*. In consequence that word is translated in our versions "sinner" and invested with an atmosphere of moral horror. Apart from the prophetic utterances it never has that meaning, but means one who is clumsy and makes mistakes, who is a blunderer by nature. It was used apparently for those who made mistakes in carrying out the ceremonial law and who thus brought upon themselves the anger of Jehovah and His priests and had to pay penalties. The transition from such angering of Jehovah to moral angering was thus easy. But in the philosophical literature it is one of the many synonyms for "fool" and means specifically the clumsy, blundering fool. Even as late as Ecclesiastes such a fool could be contrasted with the wise, prudent, rational man. But for the prophets it always involved moral horror.

The intellectualist origin of this view of sin will be plain. It is also a very modern attitude. Our most recent criminology tends to regard the criminal as mentally lacking and endeavors, usually vainly enough, to deal with him according to methods of mental therapy. The Hebrews faced the same problem but in a, for us, unhappily cynical spirit. They would probably have said that they accepted the facts of experience. Also they were burdened, from the beginning, with a feeling that man by his nature went wrong and degenerated. There was a certain élite who could profitably be helped but it was folly to try to help every one. And the evident "fool" should be let strictly alone. In Proverbs xxvi, 4, 5 two contradictory admonitions as to answering a fool are given which evidently mean, Don't answer him at all. In Proverbs ix, 7-9 the teaching is plain that the man to help is the man who is already wise, righteous and understanding. If you correct and try to help any other you will only get into trouble yourself. Yet there were differences in fools for the Hebrews, as the many synonyms show. The simpleton was easiest to help if he would only open his mind to Reason, but the clumsy blunderer and the pig-headed, self-conceited fools were hopeless. This, of course, meant a generally hopeless attitude toward what was really moral reformation, an attitude more hopeless than that of the prophets. They believed in the possibility of repentance and a change of heart because they looked at men on the emotional and religious side. But these philosophical moralists were self-righteous and cold; their methods of reform were rational admonition, and they had no understanding for deep overturnings of the moral nature. It is at this point that Hebrew philosophy contrasts most unfortunately with the deeper perceptions and warmer sympathies of the prophets whose religious ecstasies had given them a more catholic feeling for human weakness. And it was on account of this attitude that Christ forbade (Matthew v, 22) to say "Thou fool."

But it is to be remembered, also, that the Hebrews in their philosophical treatment of the nature of sin did not stop at any such lame and impotent conclusion as this. It led them to the great conception of an eternal personality, a primeval Reason, speaking to all men in all places through all the ages, a conception mystical in its origin and intellectual in its form. If evil in men is essentially Folly, then it can best be met by the Reason which exists in all God's creation and which men can find there whether as a person or not. For the Hebrews it was a person and for the Christian Church it is the personal Reason which is called the Logos in the Prologue to the Fourth Gospel.

# CHAPTER III

# REASON AMONG THE HEBREWS

THE basis of all these four positions shown in the last chapter is plainly intellectual; they do not rest on any dictum of Jehovah. They have been reached by the application of independent thought to the facts of life and at some points, even, there is a suggestion that they have been reached against the will and intention of Jehovah. That, of course, means that certain Hebrews thought that man should limit himself to the knowledge that Jehovah Himself imparts, that to seek further was impious. But it is equally plain that the Hebrews very generally did seek further and entered upon paths which led them to independent conclusions and even to conclusions critical of Jehovah Himself. Yet here, as always, it is to be remembered that the Absolute of all Hebrews, whether critics, sceptics or not, was Jehovah and that a primary object of all Hebrew philosophy was to determine His nature and not to question His existence. That short method of cutting the knot of the problem of life never occurred to them.

Yet in three at least of these four positions there is no mention at all of Reason as their basis. They are simply stated, or implied, by themselves as self-evident. This should warn us that the easy classification of certain books of the Old Testament under the rubric Wisdom Literature, that is, the regarding of these as a class by themselves and as containing what approaches toward philosophy the Hebrews made, can be very misleading. The problems which arise out of the relationship of the three separate and broad entities which the Hebrews recognized—the human race, Jehovah and the physical world—were with all the Hebrews always and affected all their attitudes and gave them stuff for thought. And it should further be observed that with the Hebrews there never took place that conversion of philosophy from the study of nature to the study of human life which in the case of the Greeks is usually ascribed to the influence of Socrates (*Phaedo*, 96-100).

Hebrew philosophy from its beginning was a study of both Nature and Man. The three existences, Jehovah, man and the non-human creation, reduce really to two, Jehovah and not-Jehovah, the Creator and His Creation, the Unseen World and the Seen World. So the Hebrew philosophy from the beginning was Man looking at and thinking about himself and Jehovah and the non-human world.

Thus the Hebrews were of necessity a thinking people and the mere fact that some of the written products of their thinking contain this word commonly translated Wisdom does not mean that no others of their writings were the product of independent thought. The early chapters of Genesis are heavy with the most subtle thinking; the Book of Jonah is a philosophical apologue of protest; often in the Psalms themselves we meet the Hebrew consciously and even grimly facing life and its problems; but this word does not occur there. Let Psalm i and Psalm ciii be read together as different phases of individual religious attitude. Behind the realistic attitude of the one and the devout attitude of the other there is a reasoned attitude toward life and much more than simple accepting and following of the command and leading of Jehovah. There is in both a conscious adjustment to the situation and to these commands. The thinkers in the two cases are concerned with different sides of life but they are both thinking. In Psalm i, just as throughout the Book of Proverbs, the thinker is somewhat crassly concerned with success in life. But in Psalm ciii it is the pathos of life and the tears of human things that are ever with the singer. Yet the whole relation between God and man is sublimated by affection, devotion and trust. The often-quoted text "Though he slay me, yet will I trust in him," is not in Job nor anywhere in the Old Testament, yet it seems the attitude of much in the Psalms. There is in it an obscured but intense feeling of the mystery of life in this world which, when the time came, was to burst into the full assurance of a spiritual life beyond the grave. The Psalmist is thinking his way under the guidance of his experiences and emotions. He is taking his mystical intuitions and reaching from them to a thought-out conclusion. His philosophy is not one of cold intellectualism but one which recognizes the eternal realities to which his emotional nature points. These facts of his experience were for him unescapable facts, bitter or sweet, and he was compelled to accept them and fit them into his tentative scheme. And so towards a philosophy of life he groped his way.

We may expect, then, to find a growing consciousness amongst the Hebrews of the existence in man's very nature of a guide as he thus gropes his way. This is not the full flood-light of authoritative revelation but something which lights each man in himself and for himself. And so we find the case.

But it is time to deal directly with the expressed attitude of the Hebrews towards Reason. They never, unhappily, separated out a specific word to be used for Reason and for Reason only. The reader of the English versions of the Old Testament will recall how often in them, and in the most varying contexts, there occurs the word Wisdom. Let him in reading these passages experiment in substituting Reason, or some similar expression such as "rational" or "thinking." He will then discover that very frequently the real meaning of the passage flashes out into new light. For the fact is that *hochmá*, the Hebrew word in question, means Reason quite as often as Wisdom. It is unnecessary to go into detail on this point here for it has been dealt with quite fully in *The Hebrew Literary Genius*, pp. 175 *ff*. The word, as is shown there, is used for any kind of mental ability or for technical skill of hand or brain. It is used, too, of animals. Thus in Proverbs xxx, 24 *ff*., ants, conies, locusts, spiders are said to possess it in a superlative degree and, contrariwise, it is said of the ostrich in Job xxxix, 17, that God has withheld it from her. In the Septuagint the word is rendered very often by σοφία, "wisdom," and that is the origin of the persistent mistranslation in our English versions. But it is also rendered by ἐπιστήμη, "knowledge," σύνεσις, "intelligence" and φρόνησις, "prudence." The Greek translators recognized the width of its usage, but it is worthy of note that νοῦς and λόγος are not used by them to represent this Hebrew word. They use λόγος very often but only in its other meaning of "word," "speech." They probably wished to avoid philosophical associations in the case of both of these words, suggesting too closely positions of Greek philosophers which all their readers must have known. Another word which is significantly absent from the vocabulary of the Septuagint is the common Greek word for skilled workman, δημιουργός. It is often needed in rendering the Hebrew, but it is always avoided. Again the philosophical usage of the Demiurge of Plato lay too close. But this applies only to the original Greek translators, whoever they were, for when we come to Philo and such writers of Jewish Greek as the author of the "Wisdom of Solomon," there is no such inhibition; Greek philosophical vocabulary and Greek philosophical ideas are used freely. That development, however, belongs to the future and took place on a foreign soil. At present all we need note is that the Greek translation must be used with the greatest caution in our attempt to understand the Hebrew text. These Greek translators in Egypt, as we shall see immediately, were more orthodox than some of the Hebrew writers and did their best to tone down and even to remove some statements which, for them, were too rash.

But we must turn to what evidence we have of the conscious consideration among the Hebrews of Reason and its place in life. First there are a few passages bearing on the relation of Reason to the authoritative will of Jehovah expressed in the very common phrase "the fear of Jehovah." A man acts according to the known will of Jehovah because he fears Jehovah. What relation does or should such action bear to action under the guidance of Reason? It is plain that the existence of Reason as an element in life was recognized, but its relative place and weight were still to be fixed. Thus in Psalm cxi, 10: "The beginning [or the principal part] of Reason is the fear of Jehovah; all that do them [apparently the commands of Jehovah] have good understanding." The word for "understanding" here is very close in meaning to our "common sense." In Proverbs ix, 10: "The beginning of Reason is the fear of Jehovah and knowledge of [about?] the Most Holy One is understanding." "Understanding" here is power of distinguishing and the word here for "beginning" can only mean "beginning." In Proverbs xv, 33: "The fear of Jehovah is the discipline of [gained through] Reason and before honor comes humility." In these statements it is plain that the object is to relate and subordinate Reason to the Authority of Jehovah. The absolute and ultimate is the command of Jehovah but man possesses in his mind a quality—reason, common sense, understanding—to aid him in the carrying out of those commands and to be a discipline for him in life. But these protests must mean that there were some who asserted that Reason was not simply an aid, or guide, or discipline, useful for the carrying out of the commands of Jehovah, but was an Ultimate of itself and in itself. That, besides the recorded Will of Jehovah, to be accepted and obeyed as Jehovah's Will, there was a guide in life, called Reason, working in and through the mind of man, which was at least of equal authority with the recorded Will of Jehovah and might even criticize that Will as it was recorded. Ultimately this meant that man could apply this Reason to the understanding and criticism of the Personality of Jehovah. We have seen the crude beginnings of this in the acquisition of a moral sense by man against the will of Jehovah and, in the end, that moral sense, guided by man's Reason, was to be applied with devastating results to the character of Jehovah. Once the conception of Reason, working as an independent instrument of investigation and applicable to all existences—God, the world and man,— was reached by the Hebrews, there was only one limit for them and a most significant limit. Jehovah might be unknowable, or He might be evil, or at least amoral, but no Hebrew, as we have seen, ever doubted that the ultimate and absolute behind existence was a personality like themselves. Apart from this single limitation Hebrew philosophy in the broad sense of the application of Reason to all life was now fully at work. When this was reached, and by what presumably gradual process, we have no clue. It shows all the signs of a normal development from the fundamental ideas which we find throughout Hebrew literature from the earliest and crudest times. More than that no one has any right to say.

The first seven verses of the fourth chapter of Proverbs give a very significant picture of how this process and development must in general have come about. It is a picture of home training and discipline; of father and mother guiding an only and beloved son. The discipline and training are rationalistic; there is nothing in them about Jehovah, or about His law and fear. But they are utilitarian and moral; the end of Reason is to be a guide in life. And the guiding is personal; father and son, teacher and pupil; all teaching means a personal teacher; until it culminates as we shall see in Reason herself as the teacher of all men. The Hebrew sense of personality is thus universalized; on the one hand is Reason, the teacher of all, and on the other is mankind who are all her Sons. No Greek ever reached a loftier conception than this of the relation of Reason to the whole human race. But its beginnings are to be found in the Hebrew father teaching his son.

> Hear, Son, the discipline of a father and give ear to the knowledge that brings understanding. For good doctrine do I give to you; my teaching reject not. For a son was I, too, of my father, tender and an only one with my mother. And he taught me and said to me, "Let thy mind hold my words; keep my commands and live. (5) Get Reason; get Understanding; do not forget nor turn aside from the words of my mouth. (6) Leave her [Reason] not, that she may guard thee; love her, that she may keep thee. (7) The beginning [or the principal part] of Reason is *Get Reason;* and in all thy gain get Understanding."

And so this moralist goes on through the rest of the chapter with no reference at all to the Fear and admonition of Jehovah; it is parental moral teaching based on the teaching of Reason. There can be no doubt that the last verse translated above is a deliberate protest against the subordination elsewhere of Reason to the Fear of Jehovah. But this was too much for the Greek translators. Verse 5 they cut down to Μηδὲ παρίδῃς ῥῆσιν ἐμοῦ στόματος, "and do not neglect the speech of my mouth," leaving out the exhortation to get Reason. Verse 7 they omitted altogether and they expanded verse 27 into a statement of the guiding power of God (ὁ θεός). Some manuscripts of the Septuagint have inserted completions of verse 5, but verse 7 occurs in no Septuagint text. We shall see hereafter how in other ways the Greek translation of Proverbs tried to preserve the absoluteness of Jehovah.

It may be well here to reiterate that the words used in the above extract from Proverbs for human reason give it as an entirely independent human capacity. How man had acquired it the Hebrew, as we have seen, did not ask. It may easily have been a sore point between the different philosophical schools and, as all admitted, in the last analysis, the absolute control of Jehovah, they may have felt that the least said the better. Not all philosophers have the courage of the Job of the Poet to go into the presence of Jehovah as an equal. The two words used here are *hochmá* and *bīna*. Of *hochmá* it is plain from the application of the root in both Hebrew and Arabic that the fundamental meaning is of controlling, directing, ruling, guiding. In Arabic, for example, a derived word means the curb or bit for a horse. Thus, for man, it is the power in him which directs and controls, exactly our Reason. *Bīna* is equally independent and absolute. It is the power which draws distinctions and therefore understands things as they essentially are. In Hebrew the two words are often used as parallels or as two ways of looking at the same thing. The words, then, could be used in this clear intellectual sense or they could be used with religious implications according to the mind and intention of the user.

The attitude in the above scrap from Proverbs is far from being irreligious. But once set rationalism freely working in the human mind and in some minds it inevitably produces an irreligious attitude. This held especially of the emotionally sardonic Hebrews with their marked feeling of personality and independence. They would go their own way, even in a spirit of mockery, and some of them did.

Of this a most singular agnostic scrap is preserved for us in Proverbs xxx, 1-4. The title by which the fragment is introduced belongs to it and is an ironical reproduction of the solemn conventional phrases of inspired utterance. It runs: "The words of Agur the son of Jakeh, the revelation, the solemn utterance of the mighty man." The Hebrew word here translated "revelation" is used regularly of the inspired utterance of a prophet, or of speech by Jehovah Himself. Literally it means "burden" and is so translated often in the English version—the Burden of Moab, the Burden of Tyre, the Burden of Nineveh, meaning the oracular, prophetic utterance concerning these places. The same is the case with the Hebrew phrase translated "the solemn utterance of the mighty man." Both words in it for "utterance" and for "man"—belong to ritual speech. Thus the phrase is used in Numbers xxiv, 3, of Balaam and in 2 Samuel xxiii, 1, of David by himself in his Last Words. This part of the title is sardonic parody of sacred language. But it is plain that more lies behind the proper names, and it is a probable conjecture, going back to old Jewish interpretation, that the two names mean "the great collector" and "the pious one." Whoever it was, therefore, that jested in this way with sacred things, expressing thereby his own agnostic attitude, he wished to put his sayings under the name of Solomon, the son of David. Similarly the author of the Book of Ecclesiastes put what he had to say in the mouth of Solomon, calling him Qohéleth, which, also, means "great collector." That Solomon was a "collector" especially of women, had impressed later Jewish thought; in that he had explicitly defied Deuteronomy xvii, 17. Indeed, some interpreters, but on another explanation of the name, held that Agur *was* Solomon.

The fragment runs:

"I have wearied myself, O God, I have wearied myself, O God, and can no more. For I am too brutish to be a man and the understanding of human kind is not mine. I have not learned reason and [so] the knowledge of [about] the Holy One how can I know? Who gathered the wind in His two hands? Who tied up the waters in a mantle? Who established all the ends of the earth? What is His name and what is His son's name—so that thou [anyone] shouldst know it?"

The meaning of this is unmistakable. The writer has no doubt that behind the world there is a Person, its creator and controller. He would probably have said that the proof of this was the existence of the world. He applies to Him the most primitive Hebrew word for God, *El.* But he can see no basis for holding that we know anything else about this being, not even that His name is Jehovah. That means that he rejects all knowledge derived from Revelation. It is only by Revelation that men know the name Jehovah and there can be no rational proof of it. His position can be paralleled in that of the scholastics of Islam. They were prepared to give a rational proof, based on the existence of the world, that the world must have had an Originator, that he must be one, eternal and other things. But as for his name, Allah, and the personal qualities ascribed to him in the Koran, these could be known only through Revelation. The same problem confronts all builders of a system of theology on a basis of pure reason. It confronted Thomas Aquinas. This Hebrew, then, has his place in the purest rationalistic tradition. But there is one obscure point in his negation and it is the allusion to a Son of Jehovah who has, assertedly, a name. This allusion calls for explanation and the explanation must be somewhat complicated. It must take in the Book of Daniel, the Book of Enoch, 2 Esdras of the English Apocrypha, often called the Salathiel Apocalypse, and Philo. It may be put thus, as shortly as possible. The sheer simplicity of the direct working of Jehovah which we find among the older Hebrews throughout our Old Testament and which, in the case of Amos, has eliminated even all angelic messengers, was evidently difficult for the later thinkers among the Jews. There must, they felt, be some intermediary, of a class above the angels, between the austere separateness of Jehovah and His creation. The frank anthropomorphism of the older Hebrews was proving too difficult for their descendants and Jehovah must be removed farther from His world. This was affecting both the Jews in Palestine and Syria who wrote Hebrew and Aramaic and the Jews in Egypt who wrote Greek. Those in Palestine and Syria show no trace of Greek philosophical influence while those in Egypt are deeply under that influence. Yet in those two developments, which may be called the Hebrew or Aramaic and the Greek, there is a common characteristic. Once we accept the postulate of the Old Testament Hebrews as to the personality of Jehovah their thinking is astonishingly sane and modern. Their attitudes are like our own attitudes and there is no touch in them of the fantastic and unreal. But when we come to the developments which seek intermediaries between Jehovah and the world, we come to thinking and attitudes which are of the highest unreality and, indeed, fantastic almost to insanity. The best example of this on the Palestinian side is the Apocalypse which is commonly called the Book of Enoch (1 Enoch, or the Ethiopic Enoch), a highly composite book of various dates by various authors, but all pre-Christian and in considerable part pre-Maccabaean. The Book consists of four separate books, but these are united in that they all purport to be the words, visions and experiences of that Enoch to whom Genesis v, 21-24 gives only four verses. Yet those four verses have intrigued all their readers since they were written. Verse 24 runs: "and Enoch walked with God and he vanished, for God took him." He had thus become a being of mystery, belonging to the Unseen World but still in his human body. So all manner of experiences could be ascribed to him; he could wander through all God's creation and receive explanations of it all and be given messages to mankind as to the future destinies of man and the world, of Israel and the heathen. This is the basis, then, and point of departure of those four books. Only one of them, however, is of special interest as to intermediaries between God and man. It is what is commonly called the Book of Parables (Enoch xxxvii-lxxi) and its author lived probably from the latter part of the second century B.C. to the middle of the first century B.C. This author had plainly been impressed by the Vision in Daniel vii, written between 167 and 165 B.C. In it God, called here the Ancient of Days, sits upon His throne in a "robe like white snow and His hair is like clean wool." To Him there came, in the clouds of heaven, a Being, described as "like a human being," and to this Being is given a universal and everlasting dominion (Daniel vii, 9, 13, 14). This seems to be the beginning of the theological phrase Son of Man which in Semitic idiom means simply "human being." The picture and phrase were taken up by this author in the Book of Enoch. He, too, has the Ancient of Days, whom he calls Head of Days and Lord of Spirits, and with hair white as wool, and also a being whom he calls similarly the Human Being. This is a personal, heavenly being who was chosen and hidden before all creation; he was given a Name before the Lord of Spirits, i.e. he was separated as a personality from the vague crowd of Sons of Elohím; he is God's Elect One and the ruler of all. He possesses righteousness in the fullest sense; his righteousness is stressed again and again and he will rule and judge in righteousness. The Spirit of Wisdom, too, dwells in him. He will be a staff to the righteous and the light of the Gentiles. He stands before the Lord of Spirits for ever and ever. Seated on the throne of his glory, he will judge the earth and destroy sinners and bring in, in righteousness, abiding peace. (Enoch xlv, 3-5; xlvi; xlviii; xlix; li, 3, 5; lii, 6, 9; liii, 6; lxi, 8-10; lxii; lxiii, 11; lxix, 26-29; lxx, 1; lxxi, 17.) In Enoch he is not called a Son, but that development may easily have been reached by Hebrew thinkers in the time of this agnostic sceptic in Proverbs. Later it was certainly reached by the writers of the highly composite book of various dates called commonly 4 Esdras, the 2 Esdras of the English Apocrypha. Throughout the book the phrase "the Son of God" keeps recurring, except in the last two chapters, xv, xvi, which appear to be a late addition. Thus in ii, 47, "it is the Son of God"; in vii, 28, 29, "my

Son, the Messiah"; in xii, 32, "the Messiah of the seed of David."
This last phrase seems to connect with a reference (iii, 24) to the
raising up of David and the command to him to build a city to the
name of the Lord and to offer oblations. But the most singular
references are in chapters xiii and xiv to "the likeness of a man"
(xiii, 3), "coming up out of the sea" (xiii, 3, 25, 51), "who had
been kept a great season," i.e. preexistent (xiii, 26). He is called
"my Son" (xiii, 32, 37, 52; xiv, 9), and the Sonship is a mystery
(xiii, 52). Here there are apparently two conceptions, a Davidic
Messiah and a quite supernatural Son; which means that the book
is very composite indeed. The central part, the Apocalypse of Salathiel, is apparently by a close contemporary of Paul and throws
light on the thinking of Paul before he became a Christian and,
also, thereafter. All this is a plain, if fantastic, development from
expressions and pictures to be found in the canonical Hebrew
Scriptures and shows no trace of Greek philosophical influence.
This Being in Enoch is called at least once "the Anointed of the
Lord of Spirits" (xlviii, 10), that is, the Messiah. He is called
"the Human Being," but is heavenly of origin as contrasted with
the earthly Messiah who is the Son of David. Was the term Son
avoided in Enoch, so as to prevent any possible confusion with
a rival conception, presenting a Son of David? Once admit a need
for some intermediary between Jehovah and mankind and the step
is not great from a Messiah who is Son of David to a heavenly
Messiah who is son of Jehovah Himself. This cannot be called
philosophy—and the agnostic philosopher in Proverbs rejects it
with scorn—but it is very free development from Old Testament
ideas. The whole picture is used of our Lord Himself in Matthew
xxvi, 64; Mark xiv, 62; Luke xxii, 69.

To the development in Egypt resulting from the mixture of
Greek philosophy with the Jewish Scriptures allusion only need be
made here. It will be taken up more fully hereafter. Its most complete expression is in Philo who was an elderly man in A.D. 40. He
was deeply affected by Platonism and his conception of God's relation to the world and of the "creation" of the world is modelled
on that in Plato's *Timaeus* (On the Creation, 15-25). Naturally,
then, the narratives in Genesis, which was inspired Scripture for
Philo, had to be treated as the freest allegory. Plato gave him also

the conception of God as a begetting father and of the world and of men as begotten by Him. This goes so far that he even (On Drunkenness, 30) represents Jehovah (ὁ θεός) as having intercourse with His knowledge (ἐπιστήμη) and so begetting created being (ᾗ συνὼν ὁ θεὸς οὐχ ὡς ἄνθρωπος ἔσπειρε γένεσιν). The conception of a divine begetting had long and sometimes very strange consequences. In the apocryphal Gospel according to the Hebrews, supposed to have stood in some relationship to the canonical Gospel of Matthew, Christ is represented as saying "My mother, the Holy Spirit" (M. R. James, *Apocryphal New Testament,* pp. 2, 5, with full references). If anything still more strangely, Aphraates, the quite orthodox Syriac Father of the fourth century, in his Homily on Virginity interprets Genesis ii, 24, of a man's leaving his father and his mother and cleaving to his wife, as a falling away from God and the spiritual life. A man's father is God, the Father, and his mother is the Holy Spirit; when he marries his mind is seduced by this world and he abandons these (Aphraates ed. Parisot, in *Patrologia Syriaca,* Vol. I, Demonstratio xviii, 10, col. 840). Philo in this was in close relation with the Neoplatonic Chain and the gnostic genealogies. But he had also close contact with the Stoic system in his doctrine of the Logos. The Stoic Logos, or Reason, is the active principle (ἀρχή) in the universe, working in the passive principle, unqualified substance (ὕλη), and is the same as God (Diogenes Laertius, VII, on Zeno, 134). God is also called νοῦς (135) and the seed-Reason of the universe (ὁ σπερματικὸς λόγος τοῦ κόσμου, 136). This Logos, meaning Reason, Philo combined with the Logos of the Septuagint, meaning Word of Jehovah. Whether he was affected in this by the Aramaic Memrá, an expression by which the Targums translated "the Word" of Jehovah and which they also personified and used to avoid crass anthropomorphisms, is very uncertain. The Memrá, it may be noted, never means Reason, although it is used for the personality of Jehovah. Thus Philo's Logos became a person, "God's Man" (ἄνθρωπος θεοῦ), who, being the Logos of the Eternal, must of necessity be himself imperishable (ἄφθαρτος—Confusion of Tongues, 41). He is incorporeal (ἀσώματον), differing in nothing from the divine image (εἰκών), eldest son (πρεσβύτατον υἱόν), first born (πρωτόγανον, 62, 63). He is the oldest of the angels, an archangel called the Beginning (ἀρχή) and the Name of God (ὄνομα θεοῦ). With the person of this Logos Philo connects the doctrine of the general fatherhood of God. Men who are yet unfit to be sons of God may be sons of this eldest-born image of God (146). That Philo's Logos was as much Reason as Word is plain throughout; cf. especially Allegorical Interpretation, I, 19.

In these two very divergent ways, of very different origins, the concept of the general fatherhood of Jehovah developed into that of His fatherhood of a single preeminent person, a Son of Jehovah. What stage this development had reached when it came to the agnostic author of the fragment in Proverbs it is impossible to say, but it may be taken as certain that he meant something more or less precise by his allusion. It was not pure rhetoric. But the allusion gave great trouble to the old translators. The Septuagint generalized it into "and what is the name of his children" ( τοῖς τέκνοις αὐτοῦ) ; the Targum, the Latin Vulgate and the Syriac have as the Hebrew ; the Arabic, dependent generally on the Greek, has actually "and what is the name of his begetter" (wālidihi), which may possibly be a corruption of waladihi, "his offspring." Otherwise it is inexplicable.

But what did this sceptic mean by the Understanding that belongs to human kind and by the Reason which separates man from the brutes? His disclaiming of these is evidently ironical; some people professed to possess them and to gain theological knowledge through them; to him they had given no such knowledge. So his denial opens before us the whole question of the place and scope, for the Hebrews, of Reason in the world. On that the Hebrews were of the most singularly divided mind, ranging from a position that human Reason was the same as God's Reason, and could read His thoughts, to one which denied that human Reason could pierce beyond the veil and which limited its scope to the mere practical conduct of life.

Of this last the most impressive and sweeping statement is in a little poem which has come down to us as the twenty-eighth chapter of Job. It was inserted, apparently, by some one who thought that it had a general bearing on the subject discussed in Job, although it has no relation at all to the structure of that Book or to the development of the argument. Its subject is, Can man attain absolute

Reason?—Reason which can reach out through the universe and read all its riddles. It is tacitly admitted in the poem that man possesses a certain rational power which guides him in his daily life. By it he can control this physical world in which he lives and draw forth and apply all its treasures to his use. The physical world belongs to man; of that there is no doubt. But at such practical things man has reached his limit; real understanding of the physical world as a whole and of its origin and essential meaning, real Reason to grasp it all in all, like Tennyson's "flower in the crannied wall"; these things are beyond man. The poem thus denies that man can reach philosophy, but such a denial means that the poet has already reached philosophy. The poem is thus the most complete vindication of the Hebrew philosophical genius. The poet feels a limitation but he looks out beyond it. Others evidently did not feel a limitation and went freely beyond this poet's barrier. And even in stating his ultimate conclusion based evidently on a theological attitude, the poet achieves a *non sequitur*; only by the use of his Reason can he dethrone Reason. Here is the summing up of his magnificent but forlorn attempt to reestablish life on a basis of ultimate Authority:

But Reason, whence does it enter and where is the place of Understanding? It is covered from the eyes of all living and from the birds of the sky it is hidden. Only Destruction and Death say, "With our ears have we heard something of it." It is God who has distinguished its way and He knows its place. For He looks to the ends of the earth; under all the Sky He sees, to give to the Wind a weight and the Waters He adjusts with a measure. When He made for the Rain a limit and a way for the Thunderbolt, then He saw it and reckoned it; He established it and also searched it out. But He said to mankind, "Lo, the Fear of Jehovah is Reason and turning from evil is Understanding."

And, so, even in this denial to man of any part in absolute Reason and assertion that for man the Fear of Jehovah is to take the place of Reason, the personality of Reason, separate from Jehovah, is asserted. And because *hochmá* is feminine in Hebrew, this personality is feminine. This became of importance as the conception of this personality hardened and Reason spoke as a mother to her sons. Jehovah saw her, examined her, used her and kept her for

Himself. This may be rhetoric, built on a metaphorical analogy—
man can find, dig out, use gold and precious stones; God only can
do that with Reason—but for the world of this poet Reason was
real, was known, was sought for and, some asserted, could be
found. And does not even the poet suggest that in the gulf and
destruction of Death man himself may attain? His phrases may be
only phrases but they make us catch our breath and wonder. This
dramatizing of Destruction and Death is great creative poetry. The
poet was trembling on a verge and seeking to save himself by holding fast to a phrase of ancient piety.

Others felt equally sure that Reason was a Person but that She
was not secluded by Jehovah and afar off. Rather She was very
close to every human being. How had this conception of Reason
as a person been reached? For the oriental all learning implies a
teacher. The student of mystical theology who has no teacher, says
an Arabic proverb, has the Devil as his teacher. In the essential
nature of every Arabic book there is implied some one to explain it
who possesses an oral explanation reaching back to the author.
Further, the innate subjectivity of the Hebrew mind came into
play. The Hebrew was so conscious of himself as a person, holding
certain ideas, sentiments, attitudes, as his own that he posited
behind all ideas, sentiments, attitudes, an individual who held them.
Every poem in Hebrew or Arabic is the formal utterance of an individual and named poet. Or, if he cannot be named, there must
come first "One unnamed has said." This affected even the gram-
matical structure of the language. In Hebrew and Arabic the "indirect speech" of the grammarian has been little developed and
used, and the "indirect question" does not exist. Statements are put
dramatically in the mouth of a speaker, as in a play. Similarly expression by an impersonal passive is rare, except to avoid, for one
reason or another, mentioning who the speaker or actor was. In the
Book of Proverbs there are many examples of this didactic direct-
ness. The exhortation is always of a person to a person, a father or
a mother to a son, or a wise man to his pupil, and the son or the
pupil is addressed personally. Once, then, Reason had been separated out as a concept the Hebrew mind would naturally posit Reason as a personal teacher of rational things. As the individual

father to his son, so would be the relation of this Reason to the whole human race. At what period separation of Reason as a concept and positing of "Her" as a universal teacher took place there seems to be no clue, but that in its beginnings it was an assertion of the rights of human reason against divine authority is highly probable. It was, in a sense, an outburst of protest. Later, different attempts were made to bring Reason into some relation to the divine personality and authority of Jehovah, and these will be dealt with below. But whoever set up "The beginning of Reason is 'Get Reason'" over against "The beginning of Reason is the Fear of Jehovah" meant what he said.

Another extremely interesting personification, to which allusion has already been made, came distinctly later than our canonical Scriptures and does not appear in the Hebrew Old Testament. It is connected with the frequent "Word" of Jehovah in the Old Testament. The Targums rendered this with *Memrá*, its literal translation in Aramaic; then this term was personified and its use extended as a means of separating Jehovah from anthropomorphic expressions which were felt to be against His dignity or spirituality. Thus it is the Memrá of Jehovah against whom man offends and it is His Memrá that "repents"; the voice of the Memrá is heard and the Memrá is put for the "hand" of Jehovah. The Memrá thus became a manifestation of God and His personified agency. But it will be noticed that this personification, both literally and in idea, connects with the authoritative Word of Jehovah. It is thus the exact opposite of the Reason of Hebrew philosophy; also it developed much later.

In at least three passages in Proverbs it is clear that Reason speaks directly. There may be other scraps among the addresses beginning "My Son" or "My Sons," but they are not clearly put into the mouth of Reason, for the dramatic, personal, form of address runs through the whole Book. But as to Proverbs i, 20-33, there can be no doubt:

> Reason without crieth shrilly; in the open spaces she utters her voice; at the head of the noisy ways she cries; in the openings of the gates, in the city, she says her says. "How long, you simpletons, will you love foolish simplicity and scoffers think scoffing

fine and the stupid hate knowledge? Should you turn to my reproof, see, I would pour out for you my spirit, I would make you
know my words. Because I cried and you refused, I stretched out
my hand and no one regarded, and you let fly all my counsel and
would have none of my reproof. I, on my part, in your calamity
will laugh. I will mock when your fear comes on you; when your
fear comes like tempest and your calamity like whirlwind; when
hostility and straits come upon you. Then, verily, they will cry to
me but I will not answer; they will seek me earnestly but they will
not find me—their return that they hated knowledge and that the
fear of Jehovah they did not choose. They would have none of my
counsel; they despised my reproof. So they shall eat of the fruit
of their way and be sated with their own counsels. For the turning
[from me] of simpletons slays them. But he that listens to me
dwells in safety and is at rest from fear of evil."

Here Reason is clearly personified and given a *mise en scène*. It is
in the busy haunts of men that her voice can be heard, if men will
but pay attention. Simpletons and the stupid she especially addresses,
but this Reason does not call them Sons. This is in truth a bad-
tempered Reason, ready to laugh and mock when misfortune comes
upon those who had refused to heed her counsels. She deals in
reproofs—the word occurs three times—and couples knowledge
and the fear of Jehovah. The Greek translation instead of "the fear
of Jehovah" has, "the word of the Lord" (τὸν δὲ λόγον τοῦ Κυρίου)
but the Hebrew is right. This Reason deals in fear and in threats.

The picture of a very different Reason is given in Proverbs ix,
1-6, 11, 12; verses 7-10 are an interpolation.

Reason has built her house; has hewn out her columns seven; has
done her killing; has mixed her wine; also has spread her table.
She has sent forth her maidens, while she [herself] cries on the
summits of the heights of the town. "Whoever is simple let him
turn aside hither." To him who is mentally lacking she says
"Come, eat of my bread [food] and drink of the wine I have
mixed. Cease, ye simpletons [from your foolishness] and live,
and go straight on in the way of understanding. For by me thy
days will be many and years of life will be increased for thee. If
thou art wise thou art wise to thine own advantage and if thou
scornest thou alone shalt bear it."

This Reason, too, cries out to all men and summons them to be taught by her under the figure of a banquet. She has built a house for herself with seven columns and she has maidens who go forth to spread her message. Stress is laid on the hewing out of the columns. All these details must have had exact meanings at which we now can only guess. The seven columns do not seem to be architectural necessities and so we are driven to conjecture an allusion to branches of knowledge. If this conjecture is correct it only makes more clear our ignorance as to Hebrew education. What, too, are the maidens of this Reason? She sends them out, but she herself does the crying in public and the summoning of men to her banquet.

Yet it may also be conjectured that this picture of Reason with her house and her banquet is a secondary contrast to the pictures that occur at least four times in Proverbs of woman as temptress and destroyer. In Proverbs ii, 16-19, she is foreign, a flatterer, and separated from her husband. She has a house but it leads straight down to Death and the Shades. In v, 3 *ff.*, she is foreign and of smooth speech and tempts men away from their lawful wives. She, too, is in her house and her ways lead to Death and Sheol. In vii, 5-27, there is a still more elaborate picture of an adulterous wife going out at night to solicit the unwary passerby and bring him to her house. And her house, too, is on the way to Sheol and leads down to the abodes of Death. The fourth occurrence is in chapter ix and comes immediately after the account of Reason and her house. It is plainly intended as a contrast and should, therefore, be translated in full, but it, too, is built on the same scheme as the other three.

> Dame Folly is turbulent, heedless and knows nothing at all. And she sits at the door of her house on a seat, high up in the town, to cry out to the passers by, to those who are going straight on their way. "If any one is simple, let him turn aside hither." And to him who is mentally lacking she keeps saying, "Stolen waters are sweet and secret food tastes well." But he does not know that ghosts are there; that her guests are in the deeps of Sheol.

Here the adulterous temptress and destroyer is turned into Dame Folly and made a contrasting figure to Dame Reason who summons men to rightness of life and safety therein. Point by point the pictures correspond or contrast, and one at least of the origins of the conception of a personified Reason is plain. The development and contrast is finally driven home by the creation of a Dame Folly. It is at least conceivable that the maidens sent out by Reason may be derived from and contrasted with less reputable girls sent out for very different purposes by some "strange woman." But no description including them has come down to us, and on the social conditions of the time we know only these pictures preserved in Proverbs.

The next great step in the personifying of Reason calls for a fresh beginning in a new chapter.

# CHAPTER IV

## THE ETERNAL REASON

THROUGHOUT the Book of Proverbs the elsewhere accepted channels of divine revelation are, to say the least, minimized. The revelation in the Mount is taken for granted, so far as the unique personality of Jehovah is concerned. There is no shadow of doubt that Jehovah is the God of Israel and has revealed Himself peculiarly to Israel. He is an overwhelming person behind everything. But practically nothing is said of the Law given in that revelation in the Mount. When the word "law" occurs in our English versions of Proverbs and is connected with Jehovah it is used in its primary sense of "teaching"—the general teaching extended on the part of Jehovah, in many ways, to mankind. The prophets, too, are ignored. There is no suggestion of the existence of such a body of men nor of the important part that they had played in the history of the people. This holds both of the organization of the prophetic guilds and of the ministry of the individual prophets. An English concordance will show this at once both as to Law and Prophets. And the contrast as to the Prophets between Proverbs and the historical books is overwhelming.

What is the nature, then, in Proverbs, of the guidance of mankind, acceptedly proceeding from Jehovah, as to faith and conduct? It is taken for granted that there is such a guidance and the guidance as exhibited is a singular compound of rather crude rationalism and a doctrine of a mystical revelation to individual men for their practical use in life. Both are based upon Reason and upon human experience, but both are dominated by the Hebrew belief in the absolute control of the whole world by the will of Jehovah. The crudely rationalistic scheme of life may be put very simply. Jehovah controls the whole world and Jehovah is "good." If, then, you wish to succeed in the world you must be "good." You will so adjust yourself to the course of the world and be successful in life. The scheme is not only crudely rationalistic but is also crudely utilitarian. Success in life is its object. This position lies behind the Book of Proverbs so generally that quotations are unnecessary.

But with it there goes a singularly subtle and lofty doctrine of an Analogy of Nature, Man and God. In it a personified Reason becomes still more explicitly a Person, who speaks as of her own authority, even apart from Jehovah, and addresses men through the phenomena of life and even of the inanimate world. Reason by her nature is rational; men as the creation—even the Sons—of Reason are rational; the structure of the world itself, which is the creation of Reason and that through which Reason speaks to men, is rational. Rationality ties up together all existent things. It is by no mere Will of Jehovah that the world is good and furthers good things; it is because the world is the creation of Reason. The appeal, therefore, of this Reason to man is somewhat changed. It is, Be rational and you will be successful. It may be urged that this is simply a repetition of the old Hebrew assimilation of the Good and the Bad to Reason and Folly. But this goes further for it is raised to a revelation which Reason herself makes to individual men, her Sons, a mystical revelation inasmuch as it comes to each man for himself. This development of the conception of the teaching Reason is revolutionary, for it practically puts Reason as a coeternal Being beside Jehovah. The conception must be in some way connected with the equally strange conception in the twenty-eighth chapter of Job of Reason as a part of the universe, found in the universe by Jehovah and taken and kept by Him for Himself. This Reason, too, which we find in Proverbs is an independent existence, but it has not been taken and kept by Jehovah for Himself. It has preserved its independence and now, in virtue of its own nature, it manifests itself to men in the scenes and operations of their daily life, calling to them to be rational as She, their Mother, is rational. We have only one statement of this conception of the personified teaching Reason, but it fits into, although going beyond, the other pictures of that Reason at its work among men. Here, as so often, we have to lament the fragmentary nature of our sources. There can be little doubt that these fragments are the remains of generations, and indeed centuries, of keen and devoted thinking on the problems raised by the phenomena of life.

This statement forms chapter viii of Proverbs:

Doth not Reason cry out and Understanding utter her voice? At the head of the heights, beside the road, between the paths, she has taken her stand. At the side of the gates, at the issue of the city, at the entry of the gateways she crieth out shrilly. "Unto you, O Men, do I cry out and my voice is directed to the sons of human kind. Understand ye, O simple ones, shrewdness and, O stupid ones, mind!

"Hear ye, for splendid things do I speak and the very opening of my lips is sincere. For trustworthiness doth my mouth murmur and the abomination of my lips is wickedness. In loyalty are all the words of my mouth; in them there is nothing tortuous or crooked. They are all straightforward to him that understandeth and straight up and down to the finders of knowledge.

"Take ye, then, my discipline rather than silver and knowledge rather than refined gold. For better is Reason than strings of jewels and there are no desirable things equal to it. For I, Reason, dwell with Shrewdness and knowing schemes do I find out. The fear of Jehovah is hating evil; so, too, do I hate pride and haughtiness with evil conduct and blatant perversities.

"Mine is counsel with effectiveness; I am understanding; mine is strength. It is by me that kings execute their office and worthy judges render true decisions. By me princes do their part and nobles—all the judges of the earth.

"I love them that love me and those who seek me diligently shall surely find me. Wealth and honor are with me—possessions abiding and true. Better is my fruit than gold—fine gold; and my increase than refined silver. In a loyal way I go on steadily through just paths, to put those that love me in possession of substance; and their treasure-houses do I fill.

(22) "It was Jehovah Himself who got me as a possession at the beginning of His course, before His works of old. (23) From eternity was I enthroned—from the beginning—from the antecedents of the earth. (24) When there were no abysses was I begotten, when there were no fountains, heavy with water. (25) When the mountains had not yet been moulded with a stamp; before the hills was I begotten. When He had not yet made the earth and the spaces beyond and the sum of the particles of the inhabited world. (27) When He established the sky, there was I; when He inscribed its circuit on the surface of the abyss; when He made firm the vault above, in hardening the water-springs of

the abyss; when He set for the sea its mark and the waters shall not pass over its edge; when He thus inscribed the foundations of the earth. (30) Then was I beside Him as a skilled workman and I was in delight, day by day, laughing before Him for every occasion, (31) laughing for His inhabited world and my delight was in the sons of human kind.

"So, now, Sons, listen to me, and oh, the happiness of those who keep my ways! Listen to discipline; be wise and reject it not. Oh, the happiness of the man who watches at my doors, day by day, while he listens to me; who guards, as it were, the posts of my doorways. For he who finds me finds Life and receives good favor from Jehovah. But he who misses me does violence to his own self; all those that hate me love Death."

The personal and separate identity of Reason could hardly be made more clear. Also the coeternity of Reason with Jehovah Himself. This is nearly an Athanasian statement, for the "begetting," if taken with its context, is almost an eternal begetting and this philosopher would probably have hesitated to say that there was, when Reason, as a Person, was not. It is true that the language is pictorial throughout and not abstract, but the idea of a divine begetting must always be pictorial. As Philo (see above) said later of the same idea—God in this acted "not as a man" ( οὐχ ὡς ἄνθρωπος ). The kernel of the conception is the statement in verse 22 that Jehovah *acquired* Reason as a possession. "Acquired" is the same word as in iv, 7, where men are told that "the beginning of Reason is, Get Reason"—get it as a possession. But that, for the translator of the Greek version of Proverbs, which is now part of the Septuagint, was too hard a saying. As he had omitted iv, 7, so here, he read, "The Lord created me" ( Κύριος ἔκτισέ με ). But other Greek-speaking Jews in Egypt did not approve of this change, for Philo twice quotes this verse as, "God obtained me" ( ὁ θεὸς ἐκτήσατό με—*De Ebrietate,* 31; *De Virtutibus,* 62). This is the rendering also of Aquila, Symmachus and Theodotion. Again, in verse 23, instead of "was I enthroned" the Septuagint reads "he founded me." ( ἐθεμελίωσέ με) using the Greek word used regularly in the Septuagint of the "founding" of the material world by Jehovah. In verse 24 "I was begotten" is omitted and in verse 25 instead of "I was begotten" the Septuagint reads "he begets me"

( γεννᾷ με ), but the other Greek versions have "I was delivered in birth" (Symmachus, ἐμαιώθην; Aquila and Theodotion, ὠδινήθην). Apparently the Septuagint translator wished to make quite clear the part in this of Jehovah. Thus, too, in verse 27, instead of "I was there" the Septuagint reads "I was present with him" (συνπαρήμην αὐτῷ ), and in verse 30 it was He who took delight in Reason and, verse 31, who "rejoiced when He had completed the world" and "rejoiced among the children of men." All this goes to minimize the separate identity and importance of Reason and to destroy Her coeternity with Jehovah.

Although it is not strictly of the present subject it may be well to throw in here that these changes had important consequences in the early Christian Church. For the Greek-speaking Fathers of that Church, the Septuagint was their Old Testament and was taken by them as inspired Scripture. Thus they could not bring together this Reason of the Book of Proverbs and the Logos of the Prologue to the Fourth Gospel. That Logos "was in the beginning with God and was God" but this Reason was a created being. So, for example, Clement of Alexandria never thought, in fact could not think, of bringing the two together. In his Exhortation to the Greeks (chapter viii, page 178 of Butterworth's edition in the Loeb Library) he quotes verse 22 in the rendering of the Septuagint as proof that God is the source of Wisdom ( σοφία ), while in chapter i of the same treatise (pp. 14 ff.) he enters at length, quoting the Prologue to the Fourth Gospel, on the doctrine of the Logos as not only the Word of God but also the Divine Reason. In consequence (p. 16) "we [men] were before the foundation of the world, we who were earlier begotten by God for the necessity of being in Him [the Logos], we who are the rational formation of the Logos of God (τοῦ θεοῦ λόγου τὰ λογικὰ πλάσματα ἡμεῖς), through whom we are of the beginning ( ἀρχαΐζομεν ) because 'In the beginning was the Logos.' " Into this view of the Logos chapter viii of Proverbs would have exactly fitted if Clement had not been misled by the "created" of the Septuagint. As contrasted with Clement's attitude, the Prologue to the Fourth Gospel is demonstrably constructed on the pattern of the eighth chapter of Proverbs. Therefore that chapter cannot have come to the writer of the Prologue in the version of the Septuagint. In what form, then, did he read it? In the Fourth Gospel there are only 21 quotations from the Old Testament as contrasted with 101 in Matthew, 56 in Mark and 86 in Luke. Of these 21 quotations a number are plainly not from the Septuagint; the writer had another source or sources for his Biblical references. But into that question this is not the place to enter.

But it was not only the Greek-speaking Jew in Egypt who had difficulty with this description of Reason. The Aramaic-speaking Jews of Palestine had difficulty also and it shows in their Targum. That Aramaic Targum does not go so far in its modifications as the Greek Targum which we call the Septuagint. It reads in verse 22 "created me" and in verse 23 "I was made firm, or established." The words in both cases could be used of the production of the material world by Jehovah. Otherwise the translation follows the Hebrew closely except that the repeated "I was begotten" in verse 25 is changed into "I was built."

This personification of Reason appears, as far as the Old Testament is concerned, only in the Book of Proverbs and in the twenty-eighth chapter of the Book of Job; where that chapter is acceptedly a quite alien insertion. In the rest of the Old Testament there seems to be no trace of this remarkable development of thought. Such a broad negative statement is, of course, precarious, but this one has been verified carefully with a Hebrew concordance. Further, in the Book of Job, although that Book is always reckoned with the so-called Wisdom Literature, the two words *hochmá* and *bīna* are comparatively rare, at least as contrasted with the Books of Proverbs and Ecclesiastes. In Job the word *hochmá* occurs only 14 times, fairly distributed between the Poet of the Colloquies, Elihu and the Speeches of the Lord. It does not occur at all in the three chapters of the Prologue and Epilogue. *Bīna,* with a synonymous word from the same root, occurs 9 times in all. It is used as a parallel to *hochmá,* with no evident difference of meaning, and *hochmá* seems to be used in general in its more exalted sense of Wisdom. But in the Speeches of the Lord (xxxviii, 36, 37; xxxix, 17) it is used, with its parallel *bīna,* in the sense, Reason. Otherwise Reason is taken for granted in the Book and the only question is whether man will or will not act with Wisdom. This apparently means that

for the various authors of the Book of Job no such emphasis upon
Reason had arisen that could possibly lead to a personification.
"Reason" was simply reason, a faculty of man which everyone
accepted without theorizing about it. We shall find this again as one
of the two attitudes in Ecclesiasticus.

In the Book of Ecclesiastes a curiously negative position is taken
up which may easily be due to conscious suppression. The author
plainly knows a great deal more as to the development of Hebrew
thought than he explicitly expresses and his readers must reconstruct freely from allusions. It is plain, too, that there was an emphasis laid in his time and environment upon the importance of
Reason—or Wisdom—and that he could not accept that importance. For him reason might be useful and even illuminating but
there was nothing ultimate about it. It was not the key to the
universe. This appears even in the formal structure of his book.
He wished to free his mind on the meaning of life in the broadest
sense and to do it in a book which would not only be a map of
life as he had found it, but also a record of himself, a confes-
sion of himself to himself. How would a thinking man, a man
of conscience and feeling, face to face with all the illogical, immoral, jumble and confusion of life, see his way through it?
How far could he really understand it and reduce it to a scheme;
how far must it remain contradictory and ungraspable? And
what should be the course of such a thinking and conscientious
man as to his own personal conduct on his way through life?
But the artistic and dramatizing instinct of the Hebrew would
not permit Ecclesiastes to put this baldly and directly as a philosophical or ethical or practical inquiry. As a beginning, at least,
he must create a figure, like the spokesman in a dialogue of Plato,
and make him propound and discuss the problem. The problem
was Ecclesiastes' own problem and was strictly a subjective one
—his own personal reactions to life—but he had to put it thus
in objective form through the mouth of a dramatically presented speaker. So the Poet of the Colloquies in the Book of Job
had put himself into Job and expressed himself through the mouth
of Job. So, too, the author of the Book of Jonah had expressed
himself still more objectively in the recalcitrant figure of the

Prophet Jonah and over his rebellious lips. Such objective presentation of the subjective is of the very essence of Hebrew art.

And for Ecclesiastes there was a mouthpiece made to his hand. The historical books of his people gave him the figure of Solomon, the Son of David, and, without doubt, the oral tradition of the people added still more of detail, edifying and unedifying. In one of those popular traditions, now otherwise lost, Solomon was called "Gatherer" (Qohéleth) and it was as a universal gatherer of all manner of experiences that Ecclesiastes thought of him. He had known life, searched it out, tested it and enjoyed it to the full. None of Adam's race had known as he the possibilities in life. And he had not been an ordinary sensualist using unlimited wealth and power to satisfy his appetites. He had been a philosopher, a poet, an administrator, a creator; he had known the secrets of nature and how to turn them to his purposes. And so Ecclesiastes evoked him from his grave, calling him by his popular nickname "Gatherer," and made him tell what life had meant for him and what its outcome had been for him.

But there lay yet more in the possibilities, for Ecclesiastes, of this historical and popular figure. He had begun life under the best religious auspices as the specific protégé of Jehovah, and he had ended it under a religious cloud, saved from the wrath of Jehovah only by the pious memory of his father David. But early in his life Jehovah had appeared to him in a dream, and as the young king, feeling the heavy burden of judging the people, asked for a mind that could hear, i.e. understand, and do justice, rather than for wealth and power, Jehovah gave him all for which he had asked and all for which he had not asked. And so he received wisdom and understanding and width of mind to grasp all knowledge. The story of this dream is told in 1 Kings iii, 5-15, and in 2 Chronicles i, 7-12. There is also a statement of Solomon's surpassing wisdom and knowledge and poetic genius in 1 Kings iv, 29-34 (in the Hebrew, v, 9-14), which the Chronicler very curiously has not taken over. Nor has he taken over the chapter of the wives and concubines and of how they led Solomon astray (1 Kings xi). Yet later Ecclesiasticus (xlvii, 14-21) refers both to Solomon's wisdom and knowledge and to the contrast between his pious youth and his dissolute age. And still later the Book of Wisdom is built entirely round the conception of an ideal Solomon ruled in all things by divine Wisdom. In any consideration of the part played by "Wisdom" in life Solomon, realistically or idealized, had necessarily to appear.

It is plain that Ecclesiastes knew these stories in Kings and Chronicles about Solomon and probably more besides. But he was also a great creative artist and understood how to work into this picture of the wise king his own experiences in life and his own conclusions about life. The result is something entirely different from the idealizing picture in the Book of Wisdom and from the stern moralizing and commonplaces of Ecclesiasticus. His figure of Solomon is a real person and is in contact with realities. And the question raised by this re-created figure—the historic Solomon illumined by the experiences of Ecclesiastes—may be put thus. What is the place of Wisdom in the life of man; what real value has it for man; can man by it reach ultimate truth and reality? In a word, did Jehovah's gift to Solomon amount to so much after all? Ecclesiastes, it is plain, did not think that it did. And his attitude on this suggests that he knew the high doctrine of Reason developed in the Book of Proverbs. Solomon, for him, had not been in contact with any such personality. Nay, more, the world was not the product of such a personality; nor were men her sons with access to her presence and to guidance by her. There was no Voice speaking through the phenomena of Nature. For man Nature was a Sphinx; its riddle he must puzzle for himself to answer; among its snares and traps he must learn for himself to walk. There is no soul in Nature for him—an empty form with empty hands—not even a unity. For the malicious care of Jehovah has elaborately constructed it out of contraries and these, too, fleeting past us. They seem to hang together, but that is only part of the scheme. This is the exact opposite of the picture in Proverbs of a world constructed by a sympathetic, loving, laughing, alluring Person, reaching out in longing to her Sons of human kind. And so, for Ecclesiastes, *hochmá*—whether Wisdom or Reason—is only the art of the prudent conduct of life. It is Life itself that man, for Ecclesiastes, has to reverence, use and cherish. But that Life is human life, a mysterious principle inherent in the race and not any life of the physical world. There is not even a mystic anodyne in Nature for him; he still holds the old Hebrew threefold division of existent things—Jehovah, man, the physical world—and for him they are separate. But a consideration of his constructive philosophy will come hereafter. Here it is enough to bring out how opposed he was to the Wordsworthian pantheism of Proverbs, so opposed as to make it almost certain that he knew that scheme. As to the practical side of life, a few quotations will make clear the strictly limited part which, in Ecclesiastes' eyes, wisdom, or reason, might be expected to play. It may be said broadly that wherever in his book a word of praise of reason enters, there follows a balancing phrase showing the limitations and the positive weaknesses in reason and in the rational attitude towards life. When the pinch comes reason breaks down; at the best, reason teaches man to bear in an understanding silence what must be borne. The facts of life ultimately are irrational. This is part of the considered policy of Ecclesiastes as a conformist. Follow no guide too absolutely, he teaches, not even reason. There are times when even folly may be in place; and there are certainly times when folly rules the world and when it is for man to adjust himself to it. And so Ecclesiastes distinguishes between a purely rationalistic attitude and an attitude of prudence and self-control. Wisdom had been Solomon's guide in life and yet he had learned that in much wisdom there was much vexation and that if you increased knowledge you increased pain (i, 18). Wisdom has something over folly as light has over darkness; the wise man has eyes in his head but the fool walks in darkness. Yet things happen to them all in the same way (ii, 13). This drives Solomon even to hate life (ii, 17); there is no ultimate advantage for the wise man. Even his wealth which he has gained he cannot secure (ii, 21-26). The wise cannot be assured of their daily bread (ix, 11), and they die even as do fools (ii, 16). Wisdom is a defense, gives life (vii, 12), strengthens (vii, 19), delivers (ix, 15), but is despised and quickly forgotten (ix, 16). All this can be verified in detail in the translation of Ecclesiastes which will come hereafter. Certainly Ecclesiastes means to exhibit Solomon discovering by experience that Jehovah's gift to him was of no ultimate value; and equally certainly there was no place in Ecclesiastes' scheme for a Reason speaking ultimate truth to man out of the original and abiding constitution of the world. It may well be that the rejection by Ecclesiastes of this high doctrine of an eternal Reason as a guide in the world, along with the stress which he lays on conformity to the order of the world, in the "fear" of God, went far to secure for him his canonical position. On these points he was "sound" and he had guarded the absoluteness of Jehovah.

The next development of the doctrine of a personified and teaching Reason in the world is to be found in the Book of Ben Sira which is commonly called Ecclesiasticus. The book has no place in the Hebrew canon of the Old Testament, although it was written by a Palestinian Jew and in Hebrew. That took place, it is now very generally accepted, about 190 B.C. Why it was not received into the Hebrew canon is a puzzle. The Book of Daniel, a compilation of a generation later, was so received. And so, too, the Book of Ecclesiastes, which is late, whatever its exact date. But Ben Sira in spite of his unhesitating piety, which is so opposed to the strict impiety of Ecclesiastes, may have failed to gain favor in his time exactly because his piety was so old-fashioned and did not recognize the new fashions of the Pharisees. He had strong affinities to the New Testament Sadducees, the conservatives of Judaism. His book was rendered into Greek in Egypt by a grandson of the author some considerable time after 132 B.C. It has come to us in a perplexing multitude of forms, often highly discrepant. There are large portions of the original Hebrew, about two-thirds of the whole, in fragmentary manuscripts of the tenth and eleventh centuries A.D., but even these do not give a uniform text; the text in the Hebrew original had come to exist in different recensions. Some of these variations go very far back and have raised the hypothesis of an expanded recension made by a disciple of the original author who had Pharisaic leanings. Similarly, and descended from these two, there are two recensions among the Greek manuscripts, one of which has very considerable additions. The version, for example, in the King James Bible is from this expanded recension and that in the English Revised Version is from the shorter form. Further there is the Old Latin version, found in the Vulgate and translated from a

Greek form, and there is a Syriac version derived directly from the Hebrew. Another Syriac version is from the Greek and there is an Arabic version mainly from the Syriac. The English reader should use the translation in the Revised Version which is a careful rendering of the shorter Greek text.

Into all this confusion and uncertainty it is impossible here to enter and also unnecessary. To reconstruct the original text of Ben Sira is an almost hopeless task and, therefore, to form a continuous and solid translation, without much citing of possible variants, is equally hopeless. Reference to any fully annotated translation will show this. But Ben Sira's broad attitudes stand out plainly and especially his antagonistic reaction to the eternal Reason of the Book of Proverbs. He carried on the old Hebrew tradition of the absolute and personal sovereignty of Jehovah and of His direct control of all that happens in the world. There is no apparent doctrine of angels as intermediaries; the one possible reference (xlii, 17) is very dubious. Some see a reference also in the Hebrew form of xliii, 26, but that is still more dubious. Ben Sira was a thorough Sadducee of the type of Amos. His doctrine of Jehovah's sovereignty led him far. After exhausting himself in xlii, 15 ff. in description of the works and absoluteness of God, he sums up with, "And the end of the matter is He is the All" (xliii, 27). There was talk among the philosophers of the time about "the All" (Ecclesiastes iii, 1). To that Ben Sira's answer is "Jehovah is the All." He certainly did not realize what he said and that his doctrine of Jehovah was leading straight to the Allah of Muslim theology who is the only Reality, and to a doctrine of the unreality of the created world. Yet with this position he combined the old Hebrew acceptance of man's free will (xv, 14-20). But this logical contradiction was no longer accepted in his time quite so easily as, for example, by Amos. The problem of the origin of the admitted evil in the world had also appeared, and Ben Sira did not feel that he could ascribe it to Jehovah as simply as the earlier Hebrews had done. He wonders how the evil element got into man's created constitution (xxxvii, 3); it cannot be from God. On the other hand the evil and destructive things in the physical non-human world are created for the vengeance of Jehovah (xxxix, 28-31).

Yet he also attempts an explanation which is much like the doctrine of Ecclesiastes that all things are in pairs, each the contrary of the other; only he does not work it out in the philosophical and critical spirit of Ecclesiastes (xxxiii, 14, 15; xlii, 24). It is plain that that doctrine, in one form or another, was a part of the thinking of his time. So, too, it is plain that he knew and accepted the stories of Creation and of the Garden in Genesis. Many references to those stories are scattered through his book and for him they were evidently solid history. Death is inevitable by the covenant from the beginning (xiv, 17; xvii, 30); man is created of the earth and returns to it (xxxiii, 10; xl, 1); and is made in the image of God (xvii, 1-3); sin and death came from Eve (xxv, 24). And so Ben Sira is in great doubt about women. A wife is necessary for complete manhood and a good wife is a helpmeet and a support. But apparently there are not many such (xlii, 9-14), and his experiences of daughters had evidently been unfortunate. It is unnecessary to accumulate references on this. He comes back to it again and again, but it does not bear directly on his philosophical position. His attitude was entirely different from that of Ecclesiastes to whom a wife could be a joy in life (Ecclesiastes, ix, 9; xii, 1). But the most important things in the life of Ben Sira were the priesthood and the Temple services (vii, 30, 31; viii, 29-31; xxxv; xlv); only do not think, he adds, to corrupt Jehovah with offerings.

And behind all Ben Sira's thought was the Law. Very strangely he gives to Ezra, the renewer of that Law, no place among the worthies of Israel, but the Law (tōrā) itself, in its precise later meaning, is the basis of his life in a way that never appears in our Old Testament. For the Book of Proverbs, as we have seen, the word tōrā means simply "teaching," but for Ben Sira it is divine legislation. With it he often combines the commandments. The most important line of family descent in the history of Israel is that of the priesthood from Aaron and Phinehas (xlv, 6-26) down to Simon son of Onias, Simon II, whom he had himself seen in his glory as High Priest. Almost the whole of the fiftieth chapter is in his praise. We realize that Ben Sira lived in the brief time when Jerusalem was ruled by the High Priests. Beside Aaron (xlv, 6-22), Moses even is given little space (xlv, 1-3), and the Davidic line still less. Aaron meant more to him than David and the restoration of the Davidic House is a very faint hope. His Messianic position is little developed. David himself was a deliverer of Israel but his permanent glory was that he sang the praises of Jehovah and ordered the Temple services and feasts and holy seasons (xlvii, 2-11). The prophets (xlviii) were great leaders and deliverers; they played their part like the good kings, David, Hezekiah and Josiah; there is no trace of a feeling for Prophecy as we know it except that Isaiah foretold "the things that should be to the end of time" (xlviii, 25), and Samuel prophesied to Saul after he was dead. In xxiv, 33, Ben Sira says of his own teaching that he will yet pour it forth like prophecy, apparently with the vehemence and assurance of a prophet. In xxxvi, 14, he prays that God may fulfil the prophecy of the restoration of Israel and in xxxix, 1, the student of Law is described as also seeking the Wisdom of the Ancients and as occupied in prophecies. In xlviii, 13, Elisha's dead body "prophesied" when it restored to life a dead man (2 Kings, xiii, 20, 31). These seem to be all the references and it is to be remembered that the Historical Books (Joshua to 2 Kings) are reckoned in the Hebrew Bible as the Earlier Prophets. According to a probable conjecture, on the basis of the Hebrew text, Ben Sira entered Job as a prophet who kept the ways of righteousness (xlix, 9). He appears to have read our Book of Job but without the least comprehension of its meaning. Fear, love and trust Jehovah whatever comes; be patient, humble and steadfast, is his teaching (ii, iii); in it we hear again the voice of Job's Friends.

Given, then, such a man as this with no feeling for the independence of the prophets as channels of influence between God and man, showing little if any feeling for the individual revelation and divine intercourse of the saint and mystic, what could for him *hochmá,* whether Wisdom or Reason, mean? Yet it is plain that the problems which this conception raised were in the thinking of the world in which he lived and that he had, of necessity, to work this conception, in some form or other, into his scheme of life and into his admonitions as to the conduct of life. For all Solomon's sensual defection his words of wisdom were part of the inheritance of Israel (xlvii, 12-20) and Ben Sira was compelled to ask himself under what guidance they were produced. In the Book of Proverbs, which he knew as part of that inheritance from Solomon, he found many different attitudes towards Wisdom and Reason. Especially he found there that picture of Wisdom, which we have already considered, as a personality coeternal with Jehovah Himself and in no relationship at all to the divine Law which had been commanded through Moses and which was carried out by the Sons of Aaron in the services of the Temple. He found there, too, an explicit separation of Reason from the Fear of Jehovah; Reason was an independent guide for men in their lives. All this was plain blasphemy to him and while he felt compelled to recognize a personified *hochmá,* whatever he thought of her, that personification had to be worked into his scheme of the divinely ordained relation between Jehovah and mankind and especially between Jehovah and Israel. For the conception in the Book of Proverbs, which he rejected, had ignored Israel and had addressed itself to all mankind.

There are especially two passages (i, 1-20, and xxiv, 1-22) in the Book of Ben Sira dealing with this conception and in them he lays stress upon the subordination of this Wisdom, upon her essential relationship to the Fear of Jehovah, upon her kinship to the Law and upon her practical identity with the Word of Jehovah. In this way Ben Sira evidently felt that it was possible, on the one hand, to recognize this new and disturbing conception and, on the other, to find an innocent place for it in the religious scheme of pious Israel.

The first of the two passages is in i, 1-20. There all *hochmá* is from Jehovah and abides with Him. And *hochmá* here we can translate quite simply as Wisdom. For Ecclesiasticus what was to be accepted by mankind and worked by them into a God-fearing life was a pious guidance which came directly from Jehovah and not this disturbing Reason which was threatening His authority. That would be Wisdom for them. This Wisdom, then, was created by Jehovah. Four times at least that is specifically said: i, 4, 9; xxiv, 8, 9. This creation was before all things and Wisdom is described as poured out upon all God's works (i, 9). It is described, too, as "rained down" (i, 19); just, as in xxiv, 3, it covers the earth like a mist. So in the creation there exists this Wisdom of

Jehovah, His free gift to all for their gladness and joy. The beginning of it is the fear of Jehovah (i, 14) ; so, too, is its fullness (v, 16) ; so, too, is its crown (v, 18) ; so, too, is its root (v, 20) ; they are all the fear of Jehovah. This goes much beyond what we have found already as to the relation of Wisdom to the fear of Jehovah. Here that fear is not only its starting point but the whole of its being. It pervades the creation, but not as a rational principle. It is divine fear and divine authority. All this is plainly built on Proverbs viii, but in such a way as to limit and correct the doctrine there.

The second important passage is in chapter xxiv, 1-22, where Wisdom herself speaks and describes and praises herself. She is, as it were, a personification of Jehovah in time and space, proceeding from Him and dwelling in and caring for His creation. But after going through all and dwelling in all she rested in Israel. In the tabernacle she abode and ministered and in Sion she was established. Her relationship, therefore, to Israel is immediate and peculiar. She came forth from the mouth of the Most High (xxiv, 3), His creative Word as in Psalm xxxiii, 6, "all the host of heaven were created by the breath of His mouth." But she also covers the earth as a mist, apparently a picture of a fertilizing mist spread over all the earth as in Psalm lxv, 12, 13, and Isaiah xlv, 8. So she proceeds from the mouth of the Most High and is spread all over the earth, working among all peoples and vivifying them spiritually. But her especial throne was in the Pillar of Cloud (xxiv, 4) and her resting place was the tabernacle (xxiv, 10) ; evidently she was the Word of Jehovah speaking to Israel. So, in Numbers xi, 25, "Jehovah came down in the Cloud and spoke to him," Moses, and in xii, 5, "Jehovah came down in the Pillar of Cloud and stood in the door of the Tent." In Psalm xcix, 7, "He was speaking to them in a Pillar of Cloud" and in Exodus xiv, 24, "Jehovah looked at the army of Egypt in a pillar of fire and cloud." At the consecration of Solomon's Temple "the Cloud" filled the House of Jehovah (1 Kings viii, 10, 11 ; 2 Chronicles v, 13, 14). See also, Exodus xl, 34, 35, and Ezekiel x, 3, 4. The Pillar of Cloud was, therefore, much more than simply a guide in the wilderness. And thus Wisdom was both universal, speaking to all men, and a special presence in Israel.

But this Wisdom, further, is identified with the Law. Immediately after Wisdom's praise of herself Ben Sira goes on (xxiv, 23), "All these things are the book of the covenant of the Most High God, the Law which Moses commanded us." Further, Wisdom is not knowledge in the broad sense, for she is the Fear of Jehovah, and the doing of the Law is in all Wisdom (xix, 20-30). This expressly rejects the idea that Wisdom is reason which knows all things and in its own light chooses for itself. Beware of those, he urges, who think that they know more than the Law. Evidently there were such in Ben Sira's time. In iii, 21-24, there is a specific warning against seeking beyond the things that have been commanded. There is no need of secret things; intellectual conceit has led men astray.

Again, men by their good deeds (iv, 10-19) can be as sons of the Most High, and Wisdom, too, has her sons whom she instructs and of whom she "takes hold" if they seek her. This is a return to the conception in Proverbs (viii, 35), "he that findeth me findeth life." In xiv, 20-27, the blessedness of the seeker of Wisdom is further developed in the tone of Proverbs. But there follows immediately xv, 1, "He that feareth Jehovah will do this and he that hath possession of the law shall obtain her," i.e. Wisdom. The Law is practically identified with Wisdom. Keep the Law and the Commandments and you will come to understand their meaning; fear Jehovah and in the end you will be wise (i, 26, 27; xxi, 11). In xviii, 1-14, there is a curious passage the teaching of which is that the works and ways of God, both His might and His mercy, are unsearchable for man. What is man's good; what is man's evil? He lives at most one hundred years and that is nothing (vs. 8, 9). Is there possibly an allusion to the fact that in the Garden Story in Genesis, which Ben Sira certainly knew and accepted, man ate of the tree of knowledge of good and evil, but not of the tree of life? In that story man would have become of the Elohím if he had eaten of the tree of life. For Ben Sira the fatal limit upon man's power and knowledge is the shortness of his life. God knows that and is merciful with all flesh. So, xvii, 30, all things cannot be in men because men are not immortal. For Ben Sira holds unshakenly the old Hebrew position that beyond death there is nothing for man. The grave is the end and there can be no praise of God there (xvii, 27). Only a good name abides (xxxix, 9; xli, 13). The dead have found eternal rest (xxii, 11; xxix, 17), but the family remains and still more the People of Israel (xxxvii, 25, 26; xli, 13).

Whether Ben Sira knew the Book of Ecclesiastes is quite uncertain, but certainly he knew the philosophical atmosphere out of which that book came. It is improbable that he really understood that philosophical group of ideas, except as tending to dangerous innovations of thought and conduct, but he certainly knew of its existence and had caught an impression from it. He had got from it the idea of all things being in pairs—a thing and its opposite—and even the expression "the All." The fear of Jehovah is the keynote of his book just as in that of Ecclesiastes, but used in an utterly different way. Did he wish, in conscious opposition, to lay stress on the real meaning of that phrase which Ecclesiastes had so parodied? We cannot tell. In xv, 20, "He hath not commanded any man to be ungodly and He hath not given any man license to sin," may be directed against such passages in Ecclesiastes as vii, 16-18. As for possible verbal echoes, x, 26, suggests Ecclesiastes vii, 16; xxvii, 26, suggests Ecclesiastes x, 8, but also Proverbs xxvi, 27; xxx, 23, suggests Ecclesiastes xi, 10. All these, however, may be proverbial commonplaces.

Further it seems plain that Ben Sira's reconstruction in orthodox terms of the idea of a personified and teaching Wisdom is an almost foreign element in his book, and, as such, it has led some students to deny the unity of the book. But the book is a plain unity with a single thinking personality behind it, and the explanation of the different conceptions of Wisdom seems to be that given here. Throughout the book in general, and especially in the latter half, Wisdom means only the practical application of the Law and the Commandments to the conduct of life; the word is an expression of such rules for life, put in keen sayings, as in the greater part of Proverbs. This is a wisdom in the minds and hearts of men; a possession of theirs which they use. But the Wisdom of Ben Sira's chapters i and xxiv is entirely different; it is the independent, coeternal Personality of Proverbs viii reduced to a creature, turned from Reason to Wisdom and worked into a scheme of Jehovah's revelation of Himself to His people. It may have been an addition by Ben Sira himself to his book when he had become convinced that the current doctrine of a personified Reason must be met and reduced to safe orthodoxy.

It is impossible to turn from a consideration of Ben Sira's book without some notice of the great contrast in personality, in attitude to life and in teaching between Ben Sira and Ecclesiastes. Whether Ben Sira knew the Book of Ecclesiastes or not, he lived in an entirely different thought-world and looked at actual life with different eyes. Life was not for him, as it was for Ecclesiastes, a primary Reality and an ultimate Good. The reality and the goodness of Jehovah, the maker and ruler and hope of all, made such a thought unnecessary. He is as cynical and worldly wise as Ecclesiastes (xiii throughout) but without the same excuse. He speaks from the point of view of the poor man who is learned in the Law (xv, 1-10) and who may be oppressed by the rich and powerful, and his ideal life is that of the scribe meditating on the Law. The scribe has chosen the better part as opposed to the always necessary workman. Yet the workman prays in his work (xxxviii, 24-39). Does not Jehovah Himself work manifoldly? It is not perfectly clear that Ben Sira actually held a School of instruction in the Law (li, 23), as has been suggested, for the phrases used are the worn formulas of the literature to which he was contributing. But he was quite conscious that he had a contribution to make (xxiv, 30-34; xxxiii, 16, 17). He might be very humble and submissive to Jehovah and the Law but he thought well of himself. So, while Ben Sira is always a schoolmaster moralizing, Ecclesiastes is a man of the world talking himself out. Both are strongly personal; they are real individual characters and show as such behind their teachings. The Book of Proverbs, on the other hand, is very impersonal and it may be conjectured—a hazardous conjecture!—that the personality of the self-confession of Ecclesiastes was a suggestion to Ben Sira. Other contrasts are plain. Between genius and decent mediocrity, although Ben Sira has passages, too, of genuine eloquence; between philosophical originality and the acceptance of a creed; between self-sufficiency with ironical submission and humility of a theological kind and a submission which is not ironical; between a rich, landed man who cares nothing for the Law, the scribes and the priests but who creates his own spiritual and moral world, and a student for whom the Law, the scribes and the priests are everything. Yet on the appalling existence of suffering in the world they were at one; both had eyes and hearts open to it although their explanations of it were entirely different. Finally, if Ben Sira had really read the Book of Ecclesiastes surely he would have spoken out upon it more clearly. To him it would have been utterly abominable. And, yet again, the specific enemy with which he wished to deal was the conception in Proverbs viii.

# CHAPTER V

## ECCLESIASTES

THE Book of Ecclesiastes has already been considered in *The Hebrew Literary Genius,* Chapter XIV. There it was treated: (i) as a psychological re-creation of Solomon and a criticism of the position tacitly assumed in the Hebrew historical writings in connection with him that "wisdom" is of primary usefulness for life in the world; (ii) as a self-confession on the part of the author; (iii) as a philosophical scheme of the universe; and (iv) as a practical guide in life. For the author himself—called here for convenience Ecclesiastes—there can be little doubt that his book was primarily a revelation of himself to himself; the evoking of Solomon from his tomb was simply an attempt at an artistic and objective *mise en scène*. But self-revelation meant the development of the author's experiences, sensations and ideas, and so he had to face a definite statement as to the nature of the world and of what lay behind the world. That he was thereby led to give practical admonitions as to life was secondary; life itself, in all its meaning and mystery, was his primary subject. His admonitions and warnings were, of necessity, very carefully balanced and were loaded against absoluteness by a fine sense of philosophical and ethical relativity. For he was in a strait between two worlds: Life with its value and glory and reality and the background of life with its rigid scheme, unchangeable except for the possible pouncing upon man of an irritable and omnipotent Personality. Rules for the conduct of life in such a universe had of necessity to be cautious to the point of immorality.

It is to that universe, as Ecclesiastes saw it and indicated it, that we must now turn, and the best introduction to his universe is a complete and faithful translation of his book. Fortunately the Hebrew text is of exceptional soundness, although it may seem, in places, harsh and jerky, as it is not always easy to guess the thought-links which the author has left unexpressed or to render the obscurities which show that he was writing in a learned language. Often the link is as much verbal as of thought. A dominant word in one section reappears in the following section even with a change of subject. It is as though he said: "Speaking of that, listen to this." Of course no translation can reproduce such connections. Words have been inserted here and there in the translation in square brackets to help out those leaps of thought and obscurities of language. Single quotation marks have also been used to indicate quoted proverbs; probably there are still more of these, as their presence can only be guessed through the context. They belong to his method of keeping connection with the past while leaving it behind. At certain points it has been necessary, mostly on the basis of the versions, to emend the Hebrew text. These emendations, however, are all very slight; the Hebraist will recognize them at once. They are not indicated here as this book is not written for the textual critic but for the student of philosophical literature. The first half of verse vii, 7, had dropped from the text before any of the versions was made. A conjectural restoration which fits the context has been inserted in the translation.

What has been said of the Book in *The Hebrew Literary Genius* is taken here as read. But it may be well to underline for the reader of this translation some of the essential words. (i) One of the most important for the thinking of Ecclesiastes was Time. The old Hebrews had no word for the abstract idea of Time. They said "days"; "in the days of" = "in the time of"; "in that day" = "at that time." But they had a word for a fixed time, or occasion, a fit season. The distinction is that between the Greek χρόνος, Time, and καιρός, occasion, season. And so the Septuagint renders Ecclesiastes iii, 1, most exactly: Τοῖς πᾶσιν ὁ χρόνος καὶ καιρὸς τῷ παντὶ πράγματι, "To all things there belongs Time and there is an occasion for every matter." Here χρόνος renders a late word which had come to the Hebrews through Aramaic from Old Persian. It occurs very seldom in the Old Testament and the Hebrews seem to have used it not absolutely but for any fixed or appointed time, practically as though it meant καιρός. But Ecclesiastes needed a word for the abstract idea, "time," and so in this one place in his book he uses this word, and his Greek translator understood him. Elsewhere in his book "time" is the other word, fixed time, occasion, season. (ii) Another word to underline is "good." Ecclesiastes, like all Hebrews, knew very well the distinction of absolute, ethical, good and bad; he took for granted that he knew these and could distinguish them. But he had another distinction. There was "good before God," that which God liked and approved, and, opposed to it, there was "blundering," something irritating to God. Inasmuch as God was amoral, this distinction was not necessarily ethical. It was a practical distinction, and the "blunderer" was really opposed to the wise, rational man, who knew better than to irritate God. This, further, illuminates Ecclesiastes' recurring phrase about "the fear of God." That did not mean, in the least, what we would call "Godly fear"; it meant caution not to irritate this amoral Personality. (iii) Another word to observe is "portion," what you get out of life as your own; or, more exactly, what God gives to you as your own. It is your "daily bread" and Islam has built up a section of theology in defining this, which it calls "sustenance." (iv) Still another recurring word indicates what is left over when something is finished, or what is a final and abiding advantage. In general, the position in this book is that nothing is ever "over" in this sense; at the end everything has been cancelled out. Again, the frequent phrases "under the sun," "under the sky," "seeing the sun" have been literally retained because they do not mean only "in this mortal life of ours on earth." Ecclesiastes had, also, a sense of joy in the sun, as is shown in xi, 7, and probably these phrases always contain a touch of that meaning.

---

I. The words of Gatherer, Son of David, King in Jerusalem.

(2) Oh, how transitory, says Gatherer, oh, how transitory, everything is transitory! (3) What is there over for Man in all his labor wherein he labors under the sun? (4) A generation goes its way and a generation arrives, but the earth forever is standing fast. (5) And the sun rises, and the sun sets, and unto its place is panting, where it is rising. (6) Going unto the south and circling unto the north, circling, circling, goes the wind and upon its circlings returns the wind. (7) All the rivers are going into the sea, but the sea is not full; unto the place where the rivers are going there they go again. (8) All things are weary—no one can express

it—the eye is not sated with seeing nor the ear filled from hearing. (9) That which has been is that which will be; that which has been done is that which will be done; and there is no new thing under the sun. (10) Is there anything that one may say, "See, this is new?" Already it was in the ages which were before us. (11) There is no remembrance of the former things, and also of the latter things, which will come, there will be no remembrance of them with those who will be hereafter.

(12) I, Gatherer, was king over Israel in Jerusalem. (13) And I gave my mind rationally to seek and to search out concerning all that is done under the skies; it is an evil toil which God has given to the sons of human kind wherein to toil. (14) I saw all the things which are done under the sun and, behold, the whole is transitory and a chasing of wind. (15) That which is crooked cannot be straight and that which is lacking cannot be counted. (16) I spoke, I to myself, thus, "I, behold, have done great things and have increased wisdom beyond all who were before me over Jerusalem, while my mind [too] has paid great heed to reason and knowledge. (17) And I have set my mind to know reason and knowledge, madness and foolishness; I know very well that this, too, is a chasing of wind, (18) for 'In much reason there is much irritability' and 'He increaseth knowledge, he increaseth pain.' "

II.    I said, in my mind, "Come, now, I will try thee with joy and do thou get thee pleasure. And behold, it was transitory. (2) Of laughter I said, "Befooled!" and of joy, "What does it accomplish?" (3) I experimented with myself to refresh my body with wine, while my mind was guiding rationally, and to hold on to foolishness up to the point where I might see what is [really] good for the sons of human kind that they should do under the skies, the numbered days of their life. (4) I made great works: I built me houses; I planted me vineyards; (5) I made me gardens and enclosures; and I planted in them all fruit trees; (6) I made me water ponds to water from them plantations of young trees; (7) I acquired men and women slaves and slaves born to me; also great possession of domestic animals, great and small, I had, above all who were before me in Jerusalem. (8) I gathered to me, also, silver and gold and the treasure of kings and provinces; I made for me singers, men and women, and the delights of the sons of human kind, concubines above number. (9) So I was great and I increased more than all who were before me in Jerusalem; also my reason stood by me. (10) And nothing for which mine eyes asked did I withhold from them; I hindered not my mind for any joy, for my mind was rejoicing because of all my labor; and this was my portion out of all my labor. (11) Then I looked carefully at all my works which my hands had done and at the labor which I had done [so] laboriously and, behold, the whole was transitory and a chasing of wind and there was nothing over under the sun.

(12) So I turned to look at reason and madness and foolishness, for what can mankind do who come after a king?— That which already has been done. (13) And I saw, I, that reason has an advantage over foolishness, of the same nature as the advantage of light over darkness. (14) The thinking man has eyes in his head, but the fool goes his way in darkness; but I indeed know assuredly that one hap befalls all of them. (15) So I said, I to myself, "As the hap of a fool so it befalls even me, so why should I be so excessively thoughtful?" So I concluded in my mind that this too, is a case of transitoriness. (16) For there is no remembrance of a thinking man just as of a fool forever; as to the already gone, in the coming days, the whole is forgotten. And how dies the thinking man? Just as the fool.

(17) Then I hated life, for an evil thing upon me was the work which is wrought under the sun, for the whole is transitory and a chasing of wind. (18) Yes, I hated, I too, all my labor in which I was laboring under the sun, because I must needs leave it to the man who should come after me. (19) And who knows whether he will be a thinking man or a fool. Yet he will have rule over all my labor and my thought. This, too, is a case of transitoriness!

(20) So, turning from this to that, I brought my mind to despair of all the labor in which I had labored under the sun. (21) For it occurs that there is a man whose labor is by reason and knowledge and ability, but to a man who has not labored in it he must give it to be his portion. This also is a case of transitoriness and a frequent evil. (22) For what comes to a man, bought by all his labor and the yearning of his mind wherein he labors under the sun? (23) For all his days are pain and vexation is his toil; even in the night his mind does not rest; this, too, is indeed a case of transitoriness. (24) There is nothing better in the case of man than that he should eat and drink and cause his self to get pleasure in his labor. I saw that this, also, is from the hand of God. (25) For who can eat and who can sensuously enjoy apart from Him? (26) For to a man who is good before Him He gives reason and knowledge and joy but to a blunderer He gives toil to add and to gather, in order to give to him who is good before God. This, too, is a case of transitoriness and a chasing after wind.

---

III. The All has Time and every event under the sky has a fit occasion:
2. An occasion of being born
     and an occasion of dying;
  An occasion of planting
     and an occasion of rooting up the planted;
3. An occasion of slaying
     and an occasion of healing;
  An occasion of tearing down
     and an occasion of building;
4. An occasion of weeping
     and an occasion of laughing;
  An occasion of mourning
     and an occasion of dancing;
5. An occasion of casting away stones
     and an occasion of gathering stones;
  An occasion of embracing
     and an occasion of holding off from embracing.

6. An occasion of seeking
    and an occasion of abandoning;
An occasion of guarding
    and an occasion of casting away;
7. An occasion of tearing
    and an occasion of sewing;
An occasion of keeping silence
    and an occasion of speaking;
8. An occasion of loving
    and an occasion of hating;
An occasion of war
    and an occasion of peace.

(9) What has the doer over through that in which he is laboring? (10) I have considered the toil which God has appointed for the sons of human kind wherein to toil. (11) All He has made suitable to its occasion; also He has put toil in their minds so that man should not find out from beginning to end the work which God does. (12) I know well that there is no good among them but to rejoice and to enjoy good in one's life; (13) and, also, that it is the gift of God for all mankind that man should eat and drink and enjoy good in all his labor. (14) I know well that all that which God does is forever; to it there cannot be added and from it there cannot be taken away, but God has done it that they should fear before Him. (15) That which has been, already it was; and that which is to be, already it has been; and God seeks [again] the dismissed.

(16) And again I considered under the sun the place of justice, thére is wickedness, and the place of righteousness, thére is wickedness. (17) I said, I to myself, "The righteous and the wicked God will judge, for He hath appointed an occasion for everything and with regard to all doing." (18) I said, I to myself, "It is on account of the sons of human kind that God may bring them out clearly, even to see that they are cattle, they in themselves." (19) For the hap of the sons of human kind and the hap of cattle—they have one hap; as one dies so the other dies, and all have one spirit; and advantage of mankind over cattle does not exist, for the

All is transitory. (20) All goes its way unto one place; all was from the dust and all returns to the dust. (21) Who knows [so] assuredly about the spirit of the sons of human kind whether it goes up, upwards [as some say], and the spirit of cattle whether it goes down, downward, to the earth? (22) So I saw that there was nothing better than that man should rejoice in his works, for that is his portion. For who will bring him in [to life again] to have pleasure in that which will be after him.

IV. But again I considered all the oppressions which are worked under the sun, and lo, the tears of the oppressed, and they have no comforter, and on the side of their oppressors there is strength, and they have no comforter. (2) So I called happy the dead, who already are dead, more than the living who are living up till now, (3) and happier than both of them [I called] those who up till now have not lived, who have not seen the evil work which is done under the sun. (4) And I saw that all labor and all skilled work means the competition of a man against his fellow—this, too, is a case of transitoriness and a chasing of wind. (5) 'A fool folds his hands and eats his own flesh'—(6) 'Better is one handful of rest than two hands full of labor,' with chasing of wind!

(7) And again I considered a case of transitoriness under the sun. (8) It occurs that there is a single man and no one with him—he has no son nor brother: but there is no end to all his labor; also his eye cannot be sated with wealth. "And for whom [he asks himself] am I laboring and depriving myself of good?" This, too, is a case of transitoriness and an evil toil it is. (9) Better are two than one, for they have a good wage through their labor. (10) For if they come to fall the one will help up his companion, but alas for him who is one [only] when he falls, and there is no second to help him up. (11) Also if two lie together they keep warm, but how can a single one keep warm? (12) A man might overcome him who is alone, but two could stand up against that man. 'And a threefold thread is not quickly snapped.' (13) Better is a poor but wise youth than a king, old and a fool,

who knows no longer how to take admonition. (14) For from the house of bondsmen he had come out to reign; for he was born in poverty, even in his own kingdom. (15) I saw that all the living, those that walk about under the sun, were with the other, the youth, who was standing in his place. (16) There was no end to all the people, to all those before whom he was. Yet those who came after had no joy in him. This, too, is a case of transitoriness and a pursuit of wind.

--------

(17) Watch thy foot when thou goest to the House of God and draw near to hear rather than [have] part with fools offering sacrifice, for they know not how to do any-
V. thing but evil. Do not hurry with thy mouth and let not thy mind hasten to bring out anything before God, for God is in the skies and thou art on the earth; therefore let thy words be few. (2) For 'Just as a dream has multitudinous toil so the voice of a fool has multitudinous words.' (3) Whenever thou vowest a vow to God delay not to fulfil it, for 'There is no pleasure in fools'; what thou vowest, fulfil. (4) It is better that thou shouldst not vow than that thou shouldst vow and not fulfil. (5) Do not permit thy mouth to bring a penalty upon thy body and say not before the Messenger [officiating priest] that it was a slip. Why should God be angry because of thy speech and ruin the work of thy hands? (6) For 'In multitudinous dreams there are both transitorinesses and words many.' But God do thou fear.

(7) If thou seest oppression of the poor and robbery of right and righteousness in the law-court, do not be astonished, for 'A high one is guarding over a high one and there are high ones over them.' (8) But the advantage of a country in everything is a king devoted to the soil. (9) 'A lover of money cannot be sated with money,' and whoever is a lover of wealth he cannot be sated with produce—this, too, is a case of transitoriness. (10) When goods increase those increase who eat them and what does the ability of their owner get except that his eyes see what he has? (11) Sweet is the sleep of a laboring man whether he eats little or much

but the satiety of a rich man does not let him sleep. (12) There occurs a sickening evil which I have seen under the sun, riches guarded for evil to its owner. (13) And that riches is lost in some evil toil [bad business] and he had begotten a son and there is not in his hand anything at all. (14) Naked as he came out from his mother's womb he goes his way again, just as he came, and nothing at all does he carry off with him, bought by his labor, that he may take away in his hand. (15) So this, too, is a sickening evil; just exactly as he comes so he goes. And what advantage has he that he was laboring for the wind? (16) Also, all his days are in darkness and mourning and much vexation and infirmity and wrath. (17) Lo, that which I have seen myself as good, that it is fitting that he eat and drink and get good [enjoy himself] in all his labor in which he labors under the sun, the numbered days of his life which God has given to him, for that is his portion. (18) Also, in the case of every man to whom God hath given riches and wealth, and authority to eat thereof, and to take his portion and rejoice in his labor, this is the gift of God. (19) For he will not greatly take thought as to the days of his life, for God keeps him occupied with the joy of his mind.

VI. There occurs an evil which I have seen under the sun and it is frequent upon man. (2) There is one to whom God gives riches and wealth and honor and he need not restrain himself from anything which he desires, and God does not give him power to eat of it [to use it], but some stranger eats of it— this is a case of transitoriness and an evil infirmity it is. (3) If a man beget a hundred and live many years, yes many are the days of his years, and his appetite is not sated with good, even though he has a burial, I say that the untimely born is happier than he. (4) For in transitoriness it enters the world and in darkness it goes its way and in darkness its name is covered; (5) also the sun it has not seen nor known; it has rest rather than he. (6) Yes, even though he were to live a thousand years, twice told, if good he did not get. Do not all go to one place? Everything goes its way. (7) All the labor of man is for his mouth and the appetite, too, can-

not be filled. (8) So what advantage has a wise man over a
fool? What has a poor man, even if he knows well how to
go about with men in life? (9) 'Better is the sight of the
eyes than the wandering of desire.' This, too, is a case of
transitoriness and a chasing of wind. (10) That which has
come to be was long ago given its name, and it is well known
that that is "Man," and he is not able to contend with Him
who is stronger than he. (11) There is indeed much talking
—mere multiplying of transitoriness. What advantage has
man in it, for who really knows what is good for man in
life—the numbered days of his transitory life? And he
passes them like a shadow. For who can tell man what will
come after him under the sun?

VII.  'Better is a good name than good olive oil'; and the day of
death than the day of one's birth. (2) It is better to go to the
house of mourning than to the house of feasting, because
that is the end of all mankind and the man who still lives
should take it to heart. (3) Better is vexation than laughter,
for by sadness of countenance the mind is better. (4) The
mind of wise men is in the house of mourning but the mind
of fools is in the house of mirth. (5) It is better to hear the
rebuke of a wise man than a man hearing the song of fools.
(6) For 'like the [crackling] sound of briars [burning]
under a pot so is the laughter of a fool.' (7) And this, too, is
transitory. [But even a wise man may fail] for oppression
can drive mad one who is wise and a bribe destroys the mind.
(8) Better is the end of a thing than its beginning; better is
the patient [low] of spirit than the proud [high] of spirit.
(9) [Yet] do not rush in thy spirit to be vexed, for vexation
rests [is permanent] in the bosom of fools. (10) Do not say,
"How did it come about that the former things were better
than these?" For it is not from wisdom that thou askest
this. (11) Wisdom is good when it is along with an inheritance and it is an advantage to those who see the sun. (12)
For 'In the shadow of wisdom, in the shadow of money'
and 'An advantage is knowledge'; 'Wisdom preserves him
who has it.' (13) Consider the work of God; for who can

make straight what He has made crooked. (14) In the time of good take the good of it, and in the time of evil consider. The one against the other has God done to the end that man may not find out anything at all after Him. (15) Everything have I seen in my transitory days: there occurs a righteous man perishing in his righteousness and there occurs a wicked man prolonging his life in his evil. (16) Be not righteous too much and do not play the wise man over much. Why shouldst thou destroy thyself? (17) Do not be wicked too much and do not be foolish. Why shouldst thou die in what is not thy occasion [of death]? (18) It is good that thou shouldst hold on to the one, but also from the other slack not thy hand; for the fearer of God will find his way out of everything. (19) Wisdom prevails for a wise man more than [any] ten rulers who were in the city. (20) For there is not a man righteous in the earth who does good and never errs. (21) Also, do not pay attention to all the things which people say, that thou mayest not hear thy slave curse thee. (22) For, also, many times thy mind knows full well that thou, too, hast cursed others. (23) All this have I tested rationally. I said, "I *will* be rational," but it was far from me. (24) Far away is that which [truly] is and deep, deep; who can find it?

(25) I turned from one thing to another, I and my mind, in order to *know,* even to search out and seek a rational reckoning and to know assuredly that wickedness is folly and foolishness is insanity. (26) And I find bitterer than death is a woman who is hunting nets [personified] and her mind is fishing nets and her hands are fetters. He who is good before God will escape from her, but a blunderer will be captured by her. (27) See, this have I found, sayeth the [present] Gatherer of one thing to another to find out a reckoning—(28) a thing which my desire still seeks but I have not found; one man from a thousand have I found but a woman in all these have I not found. (29) Only, see, this *have* I found that God made mankind straightforward, but men have sought out many reckonings.

VIII. 'Who is like a wise man and who knows the interpretation of a thing [like a wise man]?' 'The wisdom of a man illuminates his face and the strength of his face is doubled.' (2) Watch what the king says, even on account of the oath [covenant] of God. (3) Do not hasten to go away from his [angry] face and persist not in an evil thing; for all that he desires he can do; (4) in that the word of the king is authoritative and who can say to him, "What doest thou?" (5) He who does what he is commanded assuredly will not experience any evil thing and the fit occasion of judgment the mind of a wise man will surely experience. (6) For unto every thing there occurs fit occasion of judgment, for the evil of mankind is multitudinous upon him. (7) For he does not know what will come. For when it will come who can tell him? (8) As no man has authority over the wind to restrain the wind, and as there is no authority at the time of death, and as there is no discharge in war, so [in the end] wickedness will not deliver its owner. (9) All this have I observed and I have given my mind to every work which is done under the sun concerning a season when man had authority over man for evil to him. (10) And thus I saw the wicked buried in peace, but from the Holy Place those who had done uprightly must go away and be forgotten in the City; this is a case of transitoriness. (11) Because an edict as to the working of evil is not issued quickly, therefore the mind of the sons of human kind is fully set in them to do evil; (12) because a blunderer does evil a hundred times and lives long. Though also I know well that good comes to the fearers of God, who fear before Him, (13) and good does not come to the wicked who does not fear God, nor does he live long, [being] like a shadow. (14) There is a transitoriness which is done on the earth, for there occur righteous men to whom it happens like the working of the wicked and wicked men to whom it happens like the working of the righteous; I say that this also is a case of transitoriness. (15) So I, for my part, praise joy, for there is not a [real] good for man under the sun except to eat and to drink and to rejoice, it accompanying him in his labor, the days of his life which God has given to him under the sun. (16) When I gave my mind to know wisdom and to consider the toil which is done on the earth—for also, day and night, sleep with His eyes He [God] sees not—(17) then I saw all the work of God, how that man cannot find out the work which is wrought under the sun, for all that man seeks laboriously he cannot find, and even if a wise man asserts that he knows he cannot find.

IX.    So to all this I gave my mind even to make clear all this, that the righteous and the wise and their doings are in the hand of God—both love and hate—man knows not—everything is before them. (2) Everything is alike for every one. There is one hap for the righteous and for the wicked, for the good and for the bad, for the pure and for the unclean, for the sacrificer and for him who does not sacrifice; as is the good so is the blunderer; he who swears [lightly] is like him who fears [shuns] an oath. (3) This is an evil in all that which is done under the sun, that all have one hap and, also, the mind of the sons of human kind is full of evil, and madness is in their minds during their lives, and thereafter—to the dead! (4) But for whoever is [still] one with all the living there is hope; for 'to a living dog it is better than to a dead lion.' (5) For the living know that they will die, but the dead do not know anything at all, and they have no longer a wage, for their memory is forgotten. (6) Their love and their hate and their emulation have long ago perished, and they have no more a portion for ever in all that which is done under the sun.

(7) Go, eat with joy thy bread and drink with a good heart thy wine for long ago God was pleased with thy doings. (8) On every occasion let thy garments be white and oil on thy head let it not lack; (9) enjoy [*literally* see] life with a wife whom thou lovest all the days of thy transitory life which He [God] hath given to thee under the sun, all thy transitory days, for that is thy portion in life and in thy labor in which thou art laboring under the sun. (10) All that thy hand finds to do, do it with thy might, for there is

no work nor reckoning, nor knowledge, nor wisdom in Sheol, whither thou art going thy way.

(11) Again I observed under the sun that not to the light of foot was the race nor to mighty men was the battle; and, also, that not to the wise was bread and, also, not to the understanding was wealth and, also, not to the experienced was favor; for occasion and occurrence happen to them all. (12) For, also, no man really knows his own occasion; like fish taken in an evil net and like birds taken in a snare; like them are caught the sons of human kind, on an occasion of calamity when it [the calamity] falls upon them suddenly. (13) Yet this have I observed as a case of wisdom under the sun, and it was great unto me. (14) A little city, and men in it only a few, and there came against it a great king and he surrounded it and built against it great siege works. (15) But he found in it a man poor and wise, and that man delivered the city by his wisdom. And no one had had thought of that poor man before. (16) So *I* said, "Better is wisdom than might, but the wisdom of the poor man was despised and his words were not listened to." (17) The words of wise men [spoken] in quiet should be listened to rather than the shrieking of one who rules over fools [and who is, of course, a fool himself].

(18) Better is wisdom than weapons of warfare, but a
X.   single blunderer destroys much good. Dead flies corrupt and ferment the oil of a perfumer; so does a little folly to a man who is [otherwise] weighty on account of wisdom and dignity. (2) 'The mind of a wise man is to his right, but the mind of a fool is to his left.' (3) And even on the road, when a fool goes his way, his mind fails him and he proclaims to all that he is a fool. (4) If the temper of a ruler rise against thee do not give up thy place, for healing treatment will allay great blunders. (5) There occurs an evil which I have observed under the sun, of the nature of a heedlessness [slip] on the part of a ruler; [it is that] (6) Folly is set in many high places and men of wealth sit low down. (7) I have observed slaves on horses and nobles going like slaves on the ground.

(8) He who digs a pit may fall into it; and he who breaks into a wall, a serpent may bite him. (9) He who drags out stones may be put to pain by them; and he who splits logs may come into danger by them. (10) When an axe has begun to grow dull and the workman does not sharpen its edge, then he must use more strength. So the practical application of wisdom is an advantage. (11) If a serpent bites, not being charmed, he who has a tongue [can use charms] has no advantage. (12) The words of the mouth of a wise man are graceful, but the lips of a fool swallow him up. (13) The beginning of the words of his mouth is foolishness, and the end of his speech is an evil madness. (14) A foolish man, also, multiplies words, although man has no sure knowledge what will come, and what will come after him who can tell to him? (15) The labor of a fool wearies him, who does not even know how to go to the City.

---

(16) Woe to thee, O Land, whose king is of servile origin, and where nobles dine in the morning! (19) For laughter they banquet, while wine makes the joy of life and money occupies all. (17) Happy art thou, O Land, whose king is a son of freemen and where nobles dine at due season, in strength of manhood and not in drunkenness.

(18) By twofold laziness a beam sags and by slackness of the hands a house leaks.

(20) Even in thy thought do not curse a king and in thy sleeping chambers do not curse a rich man. 'For a bird of the sky will carry far the sound and a winged thing tell something.'

XI. Send away thy substance on the face of the waters, for after many days thou wilt find it. (2) Give a portion to seven and even to eight, for thou dost not know what may come, as a calamity, upon the land. (3) If the clouds are full of rain, on the land they will empty it. And if a tree falls to the south or to the north, the place where the tree falls there it is [remains]. (4) One who watches the wind will not sow, and one who gazes at the clouds will not reap. (5) Just as thou dost not know what is the way of the spirit in the bones in the womb of her with child, so thou dost not know the work of God, who does everything. (6) [Therefore] in the morning sow thy seed and at evening hold not thy hand, for thou dost not know what will prosper, whether this or that, or whether both of them, alike, will be good. (7) And sweet is the light and good it is to the eyes to see the sun. (8) So, if a man live many years let him rejoice in them all, and let him take thought of the days of darkness, for they will be many. All that comes is transitory.

(9) Rejoice [especially], O strong young man, in thy youth, and let thy mind gladden thee in thy strong young days, and go thou on in the ways of thy mind, and in the sight of thine eyes, but know thou well that, on all these things, God will bring thee into judgment. (10) So put aside vexation from thy mind and drive away evil from thy body;

XII.　for youth and the prime of life are transitory. And remember thy well of water [thy wife] in the days of thy strong youth, so long as the days of evil come not, nor the years draw nigh, in which thou wilt say, "There is nothing for me in them." (2) So long as the sun is not dark, nor the light nor the moon and the stars, nor the clouds keep returning after the rain. (3) In the day when the keepers of the house tremble, and the strong men bend themselves, and the women grinders cease working because they are few, and the women looking behind the lattices are dim, (4) and the double doors are shut to the street when the sound of the grinding is low, and he rises at the sound of birds and all the musical sounds [of his voice] are dulled. (5) Also at that which is high he fears, and terrors are in the way, and the almond tree blossoms white, and the grasshopper drags itself along, and the caper-buds fail—for man goes his way unto his eternal house and the mourners go round in the street. (6) So long as the silver cord is not snapped, nor the golden bowl crushed, nor the pitcher broken at the fountain, nor the wheel crushed into the well. (7) And the dust returns to the earth as it was, and the spirit returns to God who gave it. (8) Oh, how transitory, saith this Gatherer; all is transitory!

[(9) And, further, because Gatherer was wise he still taught knowledge to the people; and he weighed and searched; and he straightened many proverbs. (10) Gatherer sought to find pleasant words and he [also] wrote uprightly —faithful words. (11) The words of the wise are like goads and like nails, they are driven in by the members of [learned] assemblies; [but] they are given by One Shepherd.

(12) And, further, by them, my Son, be admonished. To the making of many books there is no end, and much study is physical weariness.

(13) The end of it all. Everything has been heard. God do thou fear and His commandments do thou keep; for this is all mankind. (14) For all work God will bring into judgment, concerning every hidden thing, whether good or bad.]

Ecclesiastes, like Paul, was a Hebrew of the Hebrews. But he was also an independent thinker, facing and questioning life for himself, as indeed all the old Hebrews had done. The reality of life was his strength and joy and the mystery of the background of life was his problem. His eyes were open to the phenomena of life round him; his heart was full of the pathos of life as it showed itself to him; his mind was eager to work out some consistent statement of the essential facts of life. But he was a Hebrew thinker of the primitive, sceptical, hard-headed Arab type. As a Hebrew he accepted with no shadow of doubt that behind life there was a Personality and that everything depended on the will of that Personality. This Personality was the cause of everything; was the ultimate doer of everything. So far Ecclesiastes was the orthodox Hebrew. But this Personality had erected a screen between Himself and the world, and that screen was a scheme of balanced and opposed events happening in time. These events were arranged to fit into the time of their occurrences and thus to form a connected system. The object of the scheme was to conceal God and His purposes from the prying eyes and active mind of man. God and man were essentially at strife. Man in the old story, which Ecclesiastes knew very well and, also, accepted in idea if not in historical fact, had attained, against God's will, to a knowledge of good and evil and thus had ceased to be a mere animal. But he had not attained to eternal life and, again just as in the old story, he must be kept in his place, lest he should presume further. Therefore to keep man occupied God had put into man a ceaseless drive to doing things. As the wheel of opposed events went round—each thing in its time and then its opposite in its time—man went round with it. God had imposed that upon man's mind and man could hardly help himself. It was, in fact, wisdom for man to go round with the events as they came and to conform to this scheme in which he was made a part. The events, as they came, might be harsh and difficult but man might be sure that their opposites would come in their turn and that everything would be cancelled out. This was what divine judgment had become in Ecclesiastes' sardonic thinking.

For this God of his was not in the least the Judge of all the earth who must be just, but a completely amoral being. He was the absolute source and cause of all things, but He paid no attention to moral considerations. How, then, He could have created man who —against His will, it is true—attained to a moral sense we are not told. This is the most singular defect in the thinking of Ecclesiastes. But in it he is at one with all the Hebrew thinkers and with very many modern philosophers who do not seem to reflect that they and their philosophies must be part of the universe. To this amoral character of God, Ecclesiastes was driven by what he saw in the world. There he could find no sign of a moral government; the good and the bad were handled indifferently. And so he carries the scheme of the Book of Proverbs to a very different and most ironic conclusion. God is in absolute control and rule of the world; but from the nature of the events in the world it is clear that God is amoral, does not rule on moral principles; therefore, to live successfully in the world you must be amoral also. But amoral does not necessarily mean immoral. You must be prepared to be the one or the other—be moral or immoral—as the events of the world in their contrasts require. Be the complete conformist and be ready to change when the times change. Do not be overmuch one thing or overmuch another; you will need to change and to change quickly. But man has his own sense of right and wrong, and by gaining that sense he has upset God's purposes. God had wanted man to fit into His scheme as an automaton, but man is no automaton. And there lies the danger for man. If man acts against God's carefully arranged and balanced scheme of opposites, God will strike at him right through that scheme, or screen, and destroy him. So he will die in what had not been his appointed time according to the scheme.

The Hebrew origin of all the above must be very plain. Ecclesiastes has carried out the implication which the Philosopher of Genesis preferred to leave undeveloped. He has taken the tremendous fact of the Personality of Jehovah and adjusted it to the world as he saw it. The "becoming" that lies behind all Hebrew thinking and is a fundamental characteristic of Jehovah Himself he has turned from a doctrine of perpetually new possibility to one of reiteration and return—a denial of the new. The conception of "wisdom" as a supreme guide in life he has subjected to the keen criticism of facts. For that, Solomon's Dream gave him a point of departure and also an opportunity to make Solomon himself criticize the current story of his life. And, above all, he has taken the too easy scheme of the Book of Proverbs and set it face to face with the realities of life. Thus in everything he was a Hebrew, working out from the already existent bases of Hebrew thought, looking with clear eyes at life and applying to it the acrid scepticism characteristic of the Arab mind. There was in him no touch at all of the fantastic speculations and unrealities, the coining of names and relationships meaning nothing in human experience, which mark, as we shall see, the contact of Jewish and Greek thought. His philosophy was the philosophy of a realist, of a man who, for himself, had looked steadily at life in all its manifestations and who brought over nothing from the past save the one devastating certainty that behind the passing phenomena of life there was an eternal and personal Absolute, an unknowable Will and purpose.

How, then, did he rationalize for himself these phenomena of life? His first step was to realize that they were all under the category of Time. The universe possessed Time and all the happenings in it occurred in points of time. So far as the Old Testament is concerned, this recognition of the abstract entity Time is found in Ecclesiastes only. Everywhere else in the Old Testament Time is limited to particular points or extents. We read, "at such a time," meaning a particular date; or "in the time of such and such," meaning a certain limited duration. But Ecclesiastes sees that the uni-

verse is in Time itself. Less philosophically the old Arabs before
Islam spoke of Time (*dahr*) as Fate or Fortune, because Time
brings events, good and evil, to pass. Mohammed had to tell them
that Time in this sense was Allah; He was the worker of events
and changes. In primitive Semitic thought, therefore, Time and
Fate were linked. How Ecclesiastes would have defined Time we
have no clue; but he had developed the particular "time" of the
Hebrews to this absolute conception, which is parallel to his passing from "all things" to "the All," meaning the universe. We have
no clue either as to whether Jehovah for him was in Time or, like
the Platonic Zeus, outside of Time. The screen of happenings in
Time came between man and Jehovah and so long as things ran
smoothly, as Jehovah had willed and planned them, Jehovah was
a God afar off, an absentee God, the God of the later Deists. So
far He might be thought of as out of Time. But He had retained
enough of the caprice of the God of the Semites to be irritable.
Man, in his free choice, a recognition of which is part of Ecclesiastes' Hebrew inheritance or due to his own observation of himself,
could break the sequence of the scheme and irritate Jehovah. Then
Jehovah, in His turn, would strike back in punishment into the
realm of Time.

All events, then, Ecclesiastes saw, took place in Time and each
in its own arranged time. They were adjusted to their occasions—
"beautiful" in each, is Ecclesiastes' picturesque word—and thus
smoothly followed, each the other, and made a possible whole. And
this was the more difficult because, as Ecclesiastes perceived, the
existence of each event, or happening, involved the existence of the
exact opposite of that event. If $A$, of necessity, is in the world,
there must be in the world not-$A$. This, as Ecclesiastes uses it, is
a purely philosophical conception and result. The opposed pairs in
his table in chapter iii are morally indifferent. But the origin of the
idea may easily have been ethical and apologetic and the idea itself
may, then, have been taken by Ecclesiastes and turned into pure
metaphysics. For Ben Sira has that idea in an elementary form, as
an attempted explanation of evil in Jehovah's world. The idea has
probably at many times appeared spontaneously and independently
and was evidently part of the thinking of Ecclesiastes' age. He
took it and worked it into his philosophical system. And in it he

found a complete explanation of the apparently contradictory facts
of the world. At one time there was justice and at another injustice. Both had to exist and occur because of the scheme. But people
talked of how God executed judgment on evil doers. Of course,
said Ecclesiastes, justice must come because injustice has come,
and justice, when it comes, is arranged, like everything else, so as
to fit exactly in. But injustice will also come again in its turn and
the wheel of events will go round. And so the terrible word "judgment" was stripped of all ethical quality. It was simply the sequence
of opposites. This comes out still more plainly in the advice to
strong youth at the end of chapter xi. Live fully in your youth and
strength, he admonishes, while you have them, for youth and
strength, like everything else, pass quickly away. God will bring
you into judgment for them; that is, old age will come with its
decrepitude and disability. The judgment is the physiological
change and not a moral punishment. The remembrance that it is
coming should be an incentive to fuller life, labor and enjoyment
before it comes and not a deterrent from using to the utmost the
joys and possibilities of youth. That Life must be lived, is the
greatest affirmation for Ecclesiastes; to that he returns, again and
again, even after his most despairing utterances. It might be said
that Life was his religion, the unreasoned basis of his being and
the instinctive incentive to all his action. His relation to God was
not in the least religious; it was at the most theological, a recognition of God's existence as an absolutely controlling Will behind
life. And, indeed, he had set himself, using this reality and fact of
life, to circumvent that absolute Will. His position was thus a
curious combination of Scriptural authority and psychological
observation. He accepted as fact the Garden Story in Genesis;
whether it was to him fact of idea or of history we can hardly tell.
He used it as Plato did his myths; it corresponded to the psychological and physical facts of the world as he knew them. And certainly God, for His own purposes, had imposed upon man the
necessity of toil. So man would be kept busy and God would be
secure against further encroachment. In the story the toil is physical; man must keep at work to fill his belly-need. But Ecclesiastes
in his own experience knew only the restless work of the brain; he
had never had to labor with his hands. But his brain had been

unresting and he recognized that the most real joy in life was in that ceaseless labor itself. Joy was not in the fruits of the labor but in the labor itself, in which man fulfilled his nature. So he turned the story. It was into man's *mind* that God had put labor, to the end that man should not find out the working of God as a whole. To find *that* out, Ecclesiastes saw, was hopeless, but in his own experience he realized that man could take this curse and punishment and turn it into the truest and most satisfying joy. He was by nature a worker and in working he had touched the deepest, fullest, possibility of life. Work and Life went together and Life, as has been said, was his religion. So in his book he exhorts again and again, to fill life with work, with action of one kind and another. All manner of different situations will arise; meet them, he says, each in its separate summons and need. Whatever comes do it thoroughly. But do it, too, under the control of reason and do not go too far in the doing of anything. Remember that very soon you may have to turn round and do a quite different thing. That is how God has arranged things and you must meet what He has ordained. And so there comes the paradox that Ecclesiastes, who by his own nature and code was thoroughly moral, sympathetic, honorable, was driven by the fear of God to a possibly amoral attitude. Do not be too good; do not be too bad; he who fears God will find his way out of everything. "He who fears God"—that is, he who is on his guard against God. Of such things Life is made, he would say, and man's chief end is to live Life.

Did there ever come to him a feeling that this religion of his, the living of Life, must have some reality behind it in the eternal structure and purpose of the world? That a religion which is a psychological fact in the existence of a worshiper must correspond in some way and in some degree to a metaphysical fact? That if Jehovah was his metaphysical absolute there must be in Jehovah something corresponding to this mystery of life which he felt so fully if he did not know it so well? That the description by his ancestors of Jehovah as the living God must mean something? We can only guess at answers to these questions. He was evidently writing as an old man whose physical tabernacle was breaking down and he was looking back on a youth and mature life filled with action. He had done his part by life and by his fellow men, those who had lived and walked with him "under the sun." The very reiteration of that and similar phrases means a grasping and holding on to the operations of life. And it was only with the decay of the physical possibilities of life that he was reconciled to the eternal rest and inaction of the grave. It is true that once he turned and said, "So I hated life" (ii, 17), but the very emphasis shows how dear to him life was and how full of joy. The root "to rejoice" in one form or another, and used in one way or another, occurs seventeen times in his book. But his remark which is most strangely significant for his sense of the mystery of life is in ix, 4. In one of his most melancholy passages he has testified that there is one thing which befalls all men; after all their love and hate and emulation they pass on to the dead and have no portion any more in life. Life, then, is the supreme difference, because "for whoever is still one with all the living there is *hope*." This is Ecclesiastes' one use of the Hebrew root which involves generally "trust," "reliance," "confidence." These ideas are certainly present here, but the Greek translator renders "hope," ἐλπίς, and Paul in Romans viii, 24, 25, develops characteristically Ecclesiastes' despairing recognition of the eternal hope springing in the human mind into the Christian hope ( ἐλπίς) which waits with patience even though it cannot see. The whole passage in Romans, verses 18-25, shows how Paul read, understood, developed and transcended the despair of Ecclesiastes, who could only register the inexplicable hope which he found working in his mind.

Beyond, then, the scheme which divided things into opposites and saw their certain recurrence and the recognition that life is under the category of time, Ecclesiastes' great philosophical contribution is his sense of the real existence of life, a mystery it may be, but one of the ultimate things. All the Hebrews had been vitalists whether they consciously knew it or not; their very sense of its inevitable end had sharpened the keenness of their earthly living. And when they thought of the dead lying in their separate graves they recognized that they were still alive there; they had no active life in that, their eternal house, but some kind of perception and consciousness survived. And Job could even picture himself as waiting there until God took thought of him and brought him forth from his grave to live on the earth again (Job xiv, 7-15). But

Ecclesiastes had never been on such relations of affection and trust with God, and for him his grave must be in truth an eternal house, as for the Arabs of the desert. All that was left for Ecclesiastes was this strange, new, conception of an entity, Life, which carried in it an unreasoned, even irrational, hope. This was the real essence of life and its existence seems to have been a purely psychological observation on the part of Ecclesiastes. It was a true observation and it put for him Life in the place of the Jehovah who had failed him.

Yet this life connected for him ultimately with Jehovah. Spirit, for Ecclesiastes, was the life-principle which God put into His animated creation and which He took back at death. Some asserted that there was a difference between the spirit of the lower animals which at death went down to the earth and the spirit of man which went upwards (iii, 21), but Ecclesiastes could not recognize any such distinction. This spirit was given by God and returns to God and that is a complete end (xii, 7). And this spirit evidently is the life that makes all the difference between the living dog and the dead lion (ix, 4). How, then, could Life be this strange, separate Existent—as one might almost call it—for which Ecclesiastes lived and to which he died when he died? This is the point where Ecclesiastes' psychological perception separates most markedly from the theological theory which he had taken over from the Philosopher of Genesis. He was conscious of life as a thing in itself and as a worthwhile thing, however much it might be obscured, limited and bedevilled by the God of Genesis. But the horror which this obscuring had produced was too great to carry him over the shock of death. He laid down, with relief, the burden of the disabilities of age, and saw himself in eternal rest with his fathers as the old Hebrews had always yearned to lie. So if Life was his religion, it was a religion for the living and not for the dead. And there, again, he returned to the oldest Hebrew feeling about Jehovah.

### NOTE ON ECCLESIASTES AND ARAB THOUGHT

In the half-legendary times of Arabia before Mohammed, there stands out a figure which deeply impressed the imagination of the following generations. This was Quss ibn Sá'idá, a wandering Christian preacher, called in some stories Bishop of Nejrán. If so, he was no cloistered ecclesiastic but a man who went through Arabia preaching from the back of his camel to assembled crowds at local fairs. Mohammed, even, is said to have seen and heard him at the great fair of Ukáz and to have carried the memory through all his life. And so did the rest of the Arabs; he is proverbial to this day for eloquence, poetry, wisdom and as a judge of his people. A prince-bishop, a missionary-bishop, he must have been with Arabia as his diocese. Many of the poems and sayings ascribed to him are plainly apocryphal and we can even trace their origin, but the following have a stamp of personal reality which guarantees them.

"O People, assemble, hear and remember! Who lives dies, and who dies passes away, and everything that is to come is coming. Verily, in the sky there is narration, and on the earth there is admonition—seas which move and stars which set and a roof high raised and expanses spread. . . . Allah has a religion more pleasing [to Him] than your religion which ye follow. What is there in men that they go away and return not? Are they well pleased [there] and so remain? Or do they cease and sleep—one path for all though labors diverse? In the early generations, which have gone their way, we have stuff for thoughts, since I see them going down to the wells of death, but there are none who come up again. And I see my own folk, even as they, going, little and great, and no goer returns and of those who remain there is no remnant. I am certain that I, beyond doubt, where my folk has gone, am going." (Mas'údí's *Murúj adh-dhahab,* Paris ed., Vol. I, pp. 133 *f.*)

There can be no question here of derivation from Ecclesiastes, but this is, most exactly, one side of his thought. And it is expressed in singularly compact and concrete rhyming prose. We need not imagine, however, that it gives the kernel of the preaching of this Christian missionary. The Arabs, being Arabs, were more impressed by and remembered better what agreed with their own ideas.

# CHAPTER VI

# THE HEBREWS UNDER GREEK INFLUENCE

W E TURN now to the great change which befell Hebrew philosophy when it came under Greek influence. Egypt and especially Alexandria were the melting-pot of the time; there all races and faiths and philosophies came together and had to maintain their identity and their ideas against each other or let these be modified by each other. The result produced many strange hybrids of thought and belief. In this the Hebrews had, of necessity, their part and, as we have already seen, it produced the two natural consequences, a clinging to traditional orthodoxy and a launching out into wild and speculative combinations. The Greek translation of the Old Testament, which we call the Septuagint, was produced at different times and had many authors. It is not possible here to enter upon the theological position of these separate translators, probably highly different, but we have already seen, in Chapter III, that some at least were jealously guarding the unique authority of Jehovah and considered that certain, even of the writers in Hebrew, had been lax on that point. They were willing apparently to soften for Greek ears Hebrew anthropomorphisms, but not to permit any modification, for philosophic reasons, of the foundation of their faith. On the other hand, we have already seen, in Chapters I and III, how Philo felt compelled to rationalize and Hellenize the Hebrew faith to a point where it is hardly recognizable as that of the Hebrew fathers. And varying forms of these two attitudes existed side by side.

There is no need here to enter further upon Philo. A complete study would mean a separate treatise and his general method has already been shown. His philosophical roots were in Platonism and Stoicism which were as real to him as his Jewish scriptures. They were even more real for they compelled him to destroy or evade the straight meaning of these scriptures by unlimited allegory. But that method, along with the methods of other Alexandrine Jewish writers, raises questions which must be faced. The principal one of these can be put in very direct, simple terms. How did the very sane and realistic Hebrew mind, when worked upon by the equally sane and realistic Greek mind, produce such a mass of what can only be called insane and non-realistic speculations as those of Philo and other Alexandrine thinkers? These are speculations which are not in contact with the facts of life, nor with the ideas and intuitions which naturally, for us, result from these facts. They show a singular lack of appreciation of what we certainly would call fact, whether concrete or spiritual. Out of the melting-pot of Alexandria came Philo, the Gnostics, the Neoplatonic Chain and the writers of the Hermetic tractates. There came, also, as we have seen in the case of Philo, strange semi-sexual and semi-incestuous hypotheses utterly alien to Hebrew thought and for the Greeks akin only to their old mythology. It may, perhaps, be answered that these are only metaphors, but they are metaphors stated as the expression of realities behind life and as metaphor or reality must have been deeply repulsive to normal Hebrew taste. The Hebrews, it is true, had inherited the widely spread conception of creation as a begetting but they minimized it and certainly never sexualized it. But the essential difference and fundamental trouble lay in the cutting loose of purely imaginative speculation from normal, ascertainable facts. This can only remind us of two widely separate mental phenomena of our own day, the hypotheses of our theosophists and the mathematical schemes for the universe of our physicists and astronomers.

We are compelled, therefore, to look for some explanation of this element in the different schemes of Alexandrine thought which for us means simply queerness and which carried even the realistic Jewish mind beyond itself. Was it a result of the mythological conceptions in which the Greek mind was steeped? When these ceased to have actual meaning for the Greeks as events and personalities did they turn them into philosophical abstractions? Did these abstractions then affect the Jews in Egypt as an intellectual collective hallucination? The Jews had been living for generations in the midst of an atmosphere of such hypotheses and those of them who did not hold on tenaciously to the Hebrew scriptures in their literal sense must have come gradually under strange influences. It was not simply the academic doctrines of Plato and of the Stoics which were at work but a whole environment of spiritualized mythology and realistically expressed metaphors. The Jews who remained in Palestine and clung to their Hebrew sources were not affected by this. They had cleared away all other figures from the spirit world—from their metaphysic it may be put—except the one absolute Jehovah, who was their metaphysic. The most they could do was to consider the abstract idea of the immutable and eternal truth of Reason which they had reached and find a place for it in the world. So they developed it and hypostatized it and then had to face the relation of Reason as a person to Jehovah. Their problem was a flat clashing of Reason and Authority, a situation which we at the present day understand very well and find ourselves facing. This of the Palestinians was and is a sane problem and one near to our minds, but the problems of the Alexandrines seem to us artificial and their solutions fantastically unreal. Because of the realism in the attitude of the Palestinians they had no need of allegory in their interpretations; the Alexandrine Jews were driven of necessity to allegory if they were to keep any relation at all to their sacred books.

Of these products of the Hebrew spirit in exile by far the most attractive is that commonly known as the Book of Wisdom. It is in a class by itself. It is sane in thought; it is unflinching in its adherence to the essential fact of Jehovah; it is good Greek literature; it is understanding, discriminating and sympathetic towards the world in the midst of which it was produced and to which it was intended as an appeal. For it is an apologia for the Jewish faith and the Jewish conception of the world addressed to the cultivated Greeks in Egypt. To the native Egyptians with their grotesque animal worship it is definitely hostile. The memories of the oppression in Egypt and of the terrors of the Exodus are still for the author overwhelming. He seems even to draw upon more highly colored and imaginative accounts of the oppression and the Exodus than those in his Greek Bible. But those Greeks among whom he lived, of whose civilization he felt himself a part and whose literature and ideas he knew so well were another race entirely from the Egyptians and had had no part in those old unhappy things. He had saturated himself in their literature and he liked to make allusion to it. He did this not only in the use of

Greek philosophical terms, but also in a certain literary vocabulary. An educated man in Alexandria had to know his Homer and our author evidently did. So when he refers to the Ark of Noah, with the thought of weak man at the mercy of the sea, he wishes the Greek reader to remember Odysseus and the raft he built to escape from Calypso's island (*Odyssey* v, 163 *ff.*), and calls the Ark a "raft" ( σχεδία), a word used only thrice elsewhere in the Septuagint (1 Kings v, 9 (23) ; 2 Chronicles ii, 16 (15) ; 1 Esdras v, 55) and then of rafts of logs. The perils of Odysseus gave him another rare word in the Septuagint, κλύδων, "surge" (*Odyssey* xii, 421), which our author uses twice, xiv, 5, xix, 7, the second use rather violently. From the "recesses" of the cave of Calypso (*Odyssey* v, 226) he got still another word which he alone in the Septuagint uses, μυχός, "recess," of the depths of dark night (xvii, 4) and of "the recesses of powerless Hades" (xvii, 14). It is certain that these examples could be greatly increased by comparing his vocabulary with a Homeric lexicon. The Greeks were idolaters but of a different kind from the Egyptians and for the origin of their idolatry there were possible explanations. In their philosophies there were adumbrations of the divine Unity and for their complete illumination it would be necessary to put before them only the real nature and the evident working of Jehovah.

We have thus to think of the author as a man living and thinking easily in the abstractions of Greek philosophy and ethics, but still a devout Jew. He is quite sure of the divine religious mission of the Jewish people and the personality of Jehovah is real to him. But he has no sympathy with Hebrew exclusiveness; the broad conceptions of righteousness, of truth, love, grace, mercy take him beyond the sacerdotal system. The righteous will return to rule the earth because they are righteous and not as triumphing Hebrews. The contrast of Israel and the Gentiles has given place to a contrast between the righteous and the wicked. Yet the great personified Righteousness is the Lord Jehovah.

But how could the approach be made? Zeus, he knew very well, could never lead to Jehovah; as to all the Olympians the least said the better. Their own best thinkers were ignoring them as much as the populace would permit. But there was one conception in that best Greek thinking of the time of the author which was common ground—the conception of Wisdom or Reason ( σοφία ), a conception to which all did honor and which was recognized by all as lying beyond all things and working in all things. She, this Sophia, was a reality and almost a person and the philosophers themselves, beginning with Pythagoras, in their very name as philosophers had proclaimed themselves her lovers. So the author will make this conception, Wisdom, his bridge for his heathen Greek friends to the faith of Israel. The Greek word σοφία had followed closely the same development that we have seen in the case of the Hebrew *hochmá*. It had begun as an expression for skill in handicraft and in all the arts, for judgment, intelligence, practical wisdom in life and had developed to indicate the higher knowledge in science and philosophy and so to mean profound wisdom, profound even to subtle obscurity. The wise ( οἱ σοφοί) in this sense, just like the Hebrew wise men, came to be in a class by themselves. For the Stoics σοφία was the knowledge (ἐπιστήμη) of divine and human things and of the causes of these; for Aristotle it was one of the three intellectual virtues ( διανοητικὰι ἀρεταί ) and was distinguished as "speculative" wisdom in opposition to φρόνησις, practical wisdom (*Rhetoric* I, ix, 5, 13; xi, 27). In this book φρόνησις in the practical sense "understanding" occurs iii, 15; iv, 9; vi, 15; vii, 7, 16; viii, 6, 7, 18, 21; xvii, 7. Its verb φρονέω occurs i, 1; xiv, 30 ("to think") and the cognate, φροντίζω, "to take thought on," viii, 17. Its noun φροντίς, "care for," "anxiety about," occurs v, 15; vi, 17; vii, 4; viii, 9; xv, 9. Aristotle's third intellectual virtue σύνεσις, "comprehension," "understanding," "sagacity," occurs iv, 11; ix, 5; xiii, 13, and its verb iii, 9; vi, 1; ix, 11. With all this background of technical vocabulary, which must have been familiar to his readers, our author ventures to develop the meaning of the word Wisdom ( σοφία ) along the path in which it was used in the Septuagint to represent the Hebrew *hochmá*. There, as we have seen, it was not only Wisdom but Reason, for which the Greek would have used νοῦς, and which Plato saw as of the divine nature and as divinity working in the rule of the Universe (e.g. *Laws*, Books X and XII). "Wisdom," therefore, in this book is extended to cover Reason and is the equivalent of that divine Soul (ψυχή) which is the prime mover for Plato of all things in heaven and earth (*Laws*, 897). Our author uses νοῦς only twice (iv, 12;

ix, 15) and there of the human mind in its weakness and oppressed with cares. It was for him a somewhat colorless word. But for him Wisdom, as the primary expression of the Divinity, as the working force in the world and as the appointed guide of men, was God's supreme creation and was his equivalent for the Platonic Reason and Soul. And, similarly, it is plain throughout that the human soul for him is the Platonic "soul" ($\psi\nu\chi\acute{\eta}$), the spiritual link of man with the Soul that is the prime mover of all, and not the Hebrew "soul" of our English Old Testament which expressed personality only as a center of appetites.

So our author, while he thought in Greek and used the Greek philosophical vocabulary, introduced into Greek from the development of Hebrew thought this extension of the concept Wisdom and opened the way to an enormous future development and also to much future confusion. His whole desire was to be intelligible to his Greek reading and thinking public, to men who knew their Homer and Hesiod, their Herodotus and Pindar, and who thought in the terms of Plato, the Stoics and the Epicureans. With these Wisdom, in that transcendental sense, could be his bridge and he could develop before them the personified Wisdom of his own Book of Proverbs and show to them how that conception—already, though using other words, in Plato—ran through the faith of Israel and was the soul of that faith.

But how could he create that conception before them, in dramatic imagination, as Socrates in the Platonic dialogues is represented as doing so often with his conceptions. Could he use any such figure as that of Diotima of Mantinea in the *Symposium* and make living and personal a subject which might easily lapse into arid theological controversy? Such a figure was ready at his hand. There can be little doubt that already that process had begun by which Solomon has been turned from a Hebrew king of dubious character but wide experience into a world sage. In this his dubious character had probably helped to arouse outside sympathy and interest. In his attitudes and experiences he had belonged to the world and not to Israel. That Greek world in Egypt certainly knew of him and would be glad to hear him as the spokesman of experience and of a rational theology. There may already have been mutterings of what came later to be so firmly believed, that the philosophy of

Greece was based on the wisdom of the Hebrews. Many Greeks had been willing to admit the priority of Egypt in those matters; here was a far more personal and attractive figure than anything which Egypt could vaguely furnish. He was definitely historical, too, and could be dated and had left records behind him. Less than a century earlier Ecclesiastes, for a very different audience and still more different purpose, had tried to evoke Solomon from his tomb and had only succeeded in expressing himself. There is not a scrap of evidence that our author had ever read Ecclesiastes and it is even probable that that book was not in Greek in his time, perhaps a century before Christ. But for our author, as for Ecclesiastes, Solomon as a spokesman was definitely possible, was imaginatively suggestive and so could be used to good purpose.

The very way in which that figure is used shows how well known it must have been. A characteristic of our author is an almost morbid avoidance of proper names. His book is rich in descriptive and allusive epithets but there is only one proper name in it— Pentapolis (x, 6), the Five Towns, the Cities of the Plain—and that, too, may have been meant as a descriptive. The reference to "the Red Sea" (x, 18) seems purely descriptive. In xviii, 4 and xix, 14, 15 our English translators have been compelled, for clarity, to help out obscure *"they's."* For this avoidance of names there may have been different reasons. It undoubtedly adds a certain restrained dignity to the style, as in the higher language of prayer with us where allusion is far more effective than a name. It gives the vagueness of generalization. So God has not a Throne, but thrones (ix, 11, 12; xviii, 15) and His direct presence and rule are thus spread through all things. He is enthroned everywhere. Names, too, crudely introduced, might have aroused offensive memories among non-Hebrew readers and such he wished, above all, to avoid. He may have thought, too, that in this way he was achieving a more truly Greek style. He certainly tries to build up word compounds in the fashion of Aeschylus. But where Ecclesiastes says, "I, Gatherer, was . . ." Solomon in this book says simply "I." From beginning to end his name does not occur, although it is plain that he is speaking throughout; chapters i-viii are his address to all kings and judges of the earth; chapters ix-xix are his equally elaborate address, rather than prayer, to God. It is plain, therefore, that the prefixed title, "The Wisdom of Solomon," must be taken as an integral part of the text; without it there is no speaker. And the simple occurrence of the name, in such a context, was evidently enough. But, again, knowledge of Solomon's life is taken for granted. The details of his Dream as given in 1 Kings and 2 Chronicles were not necessarily known among the Egyptian Greeks, but they knew that he, deliberately, calling upon God, chose for himself Wisdom above wealth and all other good things that he might understand the nature of things and rule and judge rightly; and that he had then found that all the good things of the world were added unto him (vii, 1-22). Solomon had this broad reputation for wisdom, knowledge and wealth in the Greek speaking world of Egypt. These Greeks may have known, too, that he had made a personal choice of Wisdom and given his life to Wisdom. Now our author is going to make him develop his reasons for that choice and show, further, the place of Wisdom in the Universe as its ultimate ruler, under God, and as the sure guide of mankind. So he will build up a great apologetic for the Hebrew race and for its faith in Jehovah, who chose it as His own people and as His mouthpiece to the rest of mankind. Solomon will show to the world that these Hebrews with their one God and their hatred of idolatry, with their cult of a righteous and moral life, with their marked racial character and customs, were no hidebound bigots or exclusive nationalists, but possessed a rational philosophy which was the very soul of their faith and which could hold its own in the world of Greek thought. One curious point in Solomon's statement is significant for the Egypt of the time and for the audience at which our author aimed. "I myself also am mortal like to all, and am sprung from one born of the earth" (vii, 1). For the native Egyptians and for the Greeks in Egypt, and even out of Egypt, it was a commonplace that wisdom and learning, the learned arts in general, were to be traced back to the teaching of the god Thoth (Θεύθ, Theuth, Tot). This god was early identified, for a variety of reasons, with the Greek Hermes. This was part of the complete confusion which arose between the Greek and the Egyptian mythologies and which is well shown in Plutarch's (*fl.* A.D. 80) tractate *On Isis and Osiris*. It is already in Herodotus. From this identification sprang much later the Hermetic writings connected with the name of Hermes Trismegistus. Thus on the Rosetta Stone (196 B.C.) "Hermes the great and great" is the Greek rendering of the Egyptian "Thoth the great-great." Solomon explicitly clears himself of any such divine claim.

A complete translation of the book which resulted from this evoking of Solomon is not necessary. That given in the Revised Version of our Apocrypha is entirely adequate, although it somewhat obscures, by the use of stereotyped theological language, the philosophical purpose of the writer. That will be seen in the scraps of translation which will follow. Nor is there, as in the case of Ben Sira, any real problem as to the text. It was written in Greek and that text has been well preserved. Nor does any elaborate analysis seem necessary here; the development of thought is clear throughout. But the purpose and method of the author and certain striking points in his argument may be brought out more fully.

First, as to his statement of God. Jehovah for him is throughout, as throughout the Septuagint, the Lord ( ὁ κύριος ). This undoubtedly meant the absolute owner and lord of all things, and was a translation of the Hebrew *Adhonay*, "my Lord," which the Jews had come to read in their Sacred Books instead of the proper name, Jehovah, or however that name was originally pronounced. But as the author of this book was writing for Gentiles he felt that further emphasis and explanation were necessary. The Greek word for God, θεός, he, of course, uses quite normally. But he strengthens the idea of absolute lordship with "the Most High." (ὁ ὕψιστος v, 15; vi, 3), "the Sovereign Lord of all" ( ὁ πάντων δεσπότης vi, 7; viii, 3), "the Sovereign Lord" (ὁ δεσπότης, xi, 26; xiii, 3), "the Sovereign Lord of these *things*," xiii, 9. In xviii, 11, "Lord," a human master, is δεσπότης as opposed to "slave," δοῦλος. Again, Jehovah is "the Almighty" ( ὁ παντοκράτωρ, vii, 25) ; His hand and word are "all powerful" ( παντοδύναμος , xi, 17; xviii, 15) ; His bounty is "all nourishing" ( παντοτρόφος, xvi, 25). He is gracious and true ( χρηστὸς καὶ ἀληθής, xv, 1) ; to be acquainted with Him is entire (*or* sound) righteousness and to know His sovereignty is the root of immortality (xv, 3). The word for "entire" or "sound" ( ὁλόκληρος ) is frequent in Plato as also that for "immortality" ( ἀθανασία ) which occurs only in this book in the Septuagint. He is "the Saviour of all" ( τὸν πάντων σωτῆρα, xvi, 7). In His works He is "the first author of beauty" ( ὁ τοῦ κάλλους γενεσιάρχης, xiii, 3), "their first maker" ( ὁ γενεσιουργὸς αὐτῶν, xiii, 5).

Those two descriptives, γενεσιάρχης and γενεσιουργός, occur only in this book in the Septuagint; the author exhausts himself to express the great first Producer. God, also, is the artificer-artist (τεχνίτης, xiii, 1) who has produced all good things; Wisdom thrice is called "the artificer of all things" (ἡ πάντων τεχνῖτις, vii, 22; viii, 6; xiv, 2). God also is "He that is" ( ὁ ὤν, xiii, 1), building on the false translation in the Septuagint of Exodus iii, 13-15. This is entirely Platonic. The Maker of the universe (Timaeus, 27 D) must be always existent, i.e. have Being and not Becoming. He is addressed "O Father!" ( πάτερ, xiv, 3) and as, "O Sovereign Lord, thou lover of souls!" (Δέσποτα φιλόψυχε, xi, 26). This shows that the "soul" for our author was the Platonic and not the Hebrew conception, and God as the first author of beauty is entirely Platonic and an echo of the discussion in Plato's Symposium where beauty leads up to the divine beauty. In sharp contrast with it is the attitude of Clement of Alexandria who has a horror of all art as leading to idolatry (Exhortation to the Greeks, Butterworth's edition in the Loeb Library, pp. 133, 141). Yet our author recognizes that art may lead to idolatry. A comparison and contrast between our Jew and Clement, both addressing the Greeks, would be fruitful.

Throughout the whole book run references to God's "production," "bringing into being" ( γένεσις ) and to the corresponding "corruption" ( φθορά) of things. This contrast is precisely in the spirit of Greek philosophy and the vocabulary used is the same. Plato in the Philebus (55 A) contrasts the two ideas and words, and also in the Laws (891 E) gives "soul" (ψυχή) as the first cause of both for all things. Aristotle wrote a treatise on "becoming" and "corruption" ( περὶ γενέσεως καὶ φθορᾶς). In the Phaedo (95 E) Socrates proceeds from this distinction of generation and corruption to his account of how he came to turn from physical science to philosophy. The distinction was indeed fundamental to Greek thinking and every educated Greek reader would understand that a book dealing with that distinction went down to the roots of things. So in this book "production" ( γένεσις ) is used a number of times of human birth (iii, 12; vii, 5; xii, 10; xiv, 6, 26; xviii, 12); also of animals and birds (xix, 10, 11); of the powers of becoming in the world (i, 14); of the beginning of creation (vi, 22); and of how Wisdom herself is the origin of all good things. Another derivative ( γεννήματα) is used of the products of a land (xvi, 19); it is curious that this same word is used in the *Timaeus* (69 C) of "the engendered sons" to whom the supreme God gives the production ( γένεσις ) of mortal things. Man is called "a product of earth" ( γηγενής) in vii, 1, and this is the word that in Plato's *Laws* (729 E) is applied to the body (σῶμα), as distinguished from the soul which is heavenly. "Corruption" ( φθορά) in a spiritual sense is ascribed in xiv, 12 to the invention of idols; that was a corruption of life itself ( φθορὰ ζωῆς) as the devising (ἐπίνοια) of them was the beginning of spiritual fornication. Through the unclean revels, too, of the Mysteries ( μυστήρια, τελεταί ) corruption was brought in (xii, 6; xiv, 15, 23 ff.), and the word "initiate" ( μύστης ) has an evil suggestion as for Plato in the *Republic* and the *Laws*. Our author associates these words with the abominations of the Canaanites, but he brings it home to his readers with the Greek vocabulary of the Mysteries. But there were also holy mysteries, mysteries of God (ii, 22), mysteries of Wisdom (vi, 22), and Wisdom is an initiate ( μύστις ) into the Knowledge of God (viii, 4). In such cases the word τελεταί does not seem to be used. On the physical side of corruption we have a corruptible body weighing down the soul (ix, 15), a corruptible thing being named a god (xiv, 8), easily corruptible creatures (xix, 20), and corruptible by fire (xvi, 27). In all these cases the word is akin to φθορά.

The kindred words for "incorruption" and "incorruptible" (ἀφθαρσία, ἄφθαρτος) are used in the Septuagint only in this book and twice in 4 Maccabees (ix, 22; xvii, 12); and the uses are significant. "Because God (ii, 23-25) created ( ἔκτισεν ) man for incorruption and made him an image of his own peculiar nature (τῆς ἰδίας ἰδιότητος); but by the envy of the Slanderer ( διαβόλος ) death entered into the world, and they that are of that one's [the Slanderer's] portion make trial of it" ( πειράζουσιν αὐτόν ; cf. i, 2). This is not an allusion to what we call the Fall but to the first recorded death, that of Abel, the cause of which was

Cain's envy. It is curious and significant that our author makes very little of the "Fall." There is the merest allusion to it in x, 1, 2, where it is said that Wisdom "guarded to the end the first formed father of the world, who was created alone, and delivered him out of his own transgression." Chapters x-xix are a record of Wisdom's benefits to the human race and this is the first of them. By Wisdom Adam was completely restored after his transgression; in xv, 8 there is, again, the merest allusion to the curse of dust to dust, suggested by the maker of *clay* ( πηλός ) idols. There is not a word about the serpent nor about Eve; Adam was created alone ( μόνος ). There is no apparent sex antagonism nor suspicion, as so strongly in Ben Sira. Our author's conventions on woman were Greek, for better or for worse, without the Hebrew depreciation or appreciation. He evidently felt that the Garden Story for his Greek audience would have little meaning, and less attraction, but saw that he could easily base the evil of the world on the grudging envy ( φθόνος ) of the great Slanderer. His Greek readers would remember the jealousy of the gods so often referred to in Herodotus (i, 32; iii, 40; vii, 46; viii, 109) and summed up in the saying "the Divinity is altogether jealous" ( τὸ θεῖον πᾶν ἐστὶ φθονερόν ). They would remember, too, the allusion to the same strange divine envy in Pindar; and in Hesiod they would remember the two strifes that among men spring from envy ( φθόνος ) and jealousy ( ζῆλος ) and vying, the one blameworthy and grudging and the other wholesome and inciting (*Works and Days*, 11 *ff.*, 195 *ff.*). They would remember, too, Aristotle's laborious analysis of the same in *Rhetoric* II, x, xi especially distinguishing between emulation and envy. But still more they would remember how in Plato's *Timaeus* (29 E) the Maker of the Universe must be devoid of envy ( φθόνος ) because he is good and desires the universe to be good like himself. So they would understand that it is not God who has envy but that great, personified, Envier and Slanderer whom they could see easily behind the word *Diabolos* which they all knew in that meaning. The phrase διάβολόν τι already meant "a touch of envy." So the Devil in this book is not, as in the rest of the Septuagint, carried over from the Satan of the Old Testament, the Adversary and Prosecuting Attorney in the court of Heaven, but is Greek and connects with the idea of supernatural envy in Herodotus and

Pindar. Envy is our author's evil principle and by it death came into
the world and corruption assailed the fair structure which God had
built up. God did not make death; He created all things that they
might live. The becomings ( γενέσεις ) of the world are full of
safety ( σωτήριοι ), without destructive poison in them, and Hades
has no kingship ( βασίλειον) on earth. The Cosmos is a champion
( ὑπέρμαχος ) of the righteous (xvi, 17), and the Creation
( κτίσις )is "screwed up" ( ἐπιτείνεται ) against the unrighteous
and "slacked off" ( ἀνίεται ) in benefaction to those who trust in
God (xvi, 24). The curious metaphor is from the tightening and
slackening of the strings of a lyre; cf. Plato's *Lysis, 209* B. The
Cosmos ministers also to God's all-nourishing bounty (xvi, 25).
The same word, "champion," occurs also x, 20 of God Himself
and evidently belonged to the usage of the time. For it occurs four
times in the Book of Maccabees of God's championing His people
and only there in the Septuagint. The older and common expression, προμαχεῖν, is used xviii, 21. Righteousness—perfectly righteous men—are immortal; but the wicked by their deeds and words
draw Hades to them. So we may fairly render i, 13-16 and see the
problem of death and evil and corruption as our author saw it in
his own faith and tried to make it plain to his Greek readers. He
returns again to Envy in vi, 23, where he makes Solomon say that
he will not be restrained by "envy that wastes away," i.e. is useless
and negative, from putting the knowledge and the riches of Wisdom
before his fellow kings and judges of the earth. The expression is
φθόνῳ τετηκότι and the verb is used several times in the book
(i, 16; xvi, 22, 27, 29) in the sense "consume away," "melt away";
it is quite common in Homer in the sense "waste away" with dis-
ease or sorrow, and this expression may be built, as elsewhere in
this book, on an Homeric recollection.

It is worth noticing, further, as to the relation of this book to
Greek literary usage, that its word for "envy," φθόνος, never
occurs in the parts of the Septuagint which are translated from our
Hebrew Old Testament and rarely in the Septuagint elsewhere. It
is in the Greek translation of Ben Sira (xiv, 10) and in Tobit (iv,
16) for an evil or grudging eye. It is also, in 1 Maccabees viii, 16
coupled with ζῆλος, envy and emulation, but that is all. When our
author, however, uses the word ζῆλος, ζήλωσις or its verb ζηλοῦν

(i, 10, 12; v, 18) it is in the sense of the Hebrew *qin'a,* "zeal," "fervency" and not in the Aristotelian sense of "praiseworthy" emulation, to be distinguished from evil "envy." He knew very well what he was doing in his use of φθόνος and in his reference, which all must have understood, to the envy of the gods. He uses it again in vii, 13, where Solomon says, "without guile I learned and without grudging ( ἀφθόνως ) I teach." This form, too, does not occur elsewhere in the Septuagint. It may be added that the conception of "envy," expressed in this same word, continued in Egyptian religious thought and reappears in the Hermetic writings in the second and third Christian centuries (Lib. iv, 3), apparently derived from the *Timaeus.*

Behind "production" or "becoming" and "corruption" lies "creation" in whatever exact sense that word is meant. For it our author used κτίζω, one of the two words used most commonly in the Septuagint to render the Hebrew word usually translated "create" in our Version. It was evidently in common use among Alexandrian Jews in that sense as the Greek translator of Ben Sira uses it, or words derived from it, twenty-seven times. It is the word used also in the Greek version of Proverbs viii, 22, to mistranslate (Chapter IV above) "God got me as a possession." This usage was Scripture for our author and affected, as we shall see, his doctrine of Wisdom. He uses this verb five times (i, 14; ii, 23; x, 1; xi, 18; xiii, 3). Three of these have already been translated; i, 14 runs, "for he created all things that they might have being" (εἰς τὸ εἶναι); xi, 18, "created the world out of formless matter" ( ἐξ ἀμόρφου ὕλης), which shows how he understood "creation." The noun "creation" ( κτίσις ) occurs ii, 6; v, 17; xvi, 24; xix, 6, and the noun "creature" ( κτίσμα ) ix, 2; xiii, 5; xiv, 11. The verb κτίζω is perfectly good classical Greek, used by Herodotus, Thucydides, Pindar, the dramatists, in the senses, to people a country, found a city, build a home, establish, produce, but it does not seem to have had philosophical usage. Our author used another good classical verb κατασκευάζω (to equip, build, establish, form), for divine formative working. It occurs, xiii, 11, of a skilled workman forming a vessel useful for the service of life. But in vii, 27 Wisdom equips men to be friends of God and prophets, and, ix, 2, "by thy Wisdom thou (God) equippedst man to rule over the creatures." The phrase "friends of God" (φίλους θεοῦ) is said not to occur elsewhere in the Septuagint, but friendship between God and man was deeply implanted in the Hebrew mind. Kindness (Hebrew *hésedh*) existed not only from God to man but from man to God. The Greek readers of this book would remember the same phrase used by Xenophon, Plato, Epictetus and Diogenes. They would remember, too, that prophets (προφῆται, *Timaeus, 72*) were interpreters of what was given in inspired divination (μαντεία). In xi, 24 it is said of God, "for thou lovest all beings and hatest none of those whom thou hast made (ἐποίησας) for never, while hating, wouldst thou have formed (κατεσκεύασας) anything." All God's creation is an expression of love and never of hate; it is the voice of Plato that we hear. In xiii, 4 there is a similar echo; "let them understand from them [the good and beautiful works of God] how much more powerful is he who formed them." So Plato, from the army of unalterable law in the heavens deduced the rule of justice and kindness and goodness on the earth.

We can now return to the conception of incorruption in God's creation. In vi, 18, 19 Wisdom and incorruption are linked. "Love [of Wisdom] is observance of her laws and attention to her laws is a warranty [a legal term] of incorruption, and incorruption works being near to God." Obedience to Wisdom does not confer incorruption but guarantees it. Men are born to incorruption and thus to nearness to God but they may of their own will put it from them. Again in xi, 26-xii, 1, "thou sparest all things because they are thine, O Sovereign Lord, Lover of Souls, for thine incorruptible spirit is in all things." God has a spirit that has filled the world and holds all things together (i, 7); so exactly the Stoics, too, held. This spirit is holy (ἁγιόν); "But thy counsel who knew except thou gavest wisdom and didst send thy holy spirit from on high" (ix, 17). The last of the references to incorruption in the divine working is in xviii, 4, with which verse 9 must be taken. "Thy sons through whom the incorruptible light of the law was to be given to the world" (αἰών). . . . "With unanimity they took upon themselves the law of the divine nature" (θειότης). This is the only occurrence of θειότης in the Septuagint but it is used several times by Plutarch in its etymological sense "divinity," "divine nature." Here we have the incorruptible light of God's revelation to Israel of

Himself which Israel is to give to the world and which is the law, or rule, of the divine nature. Law ( νόμος ), here, should not be taken in the technical sense of the ritual Law of Moses. Our author has no reference to that and cared little for it; in iii, 14, he contradicts it flatly. When he uses the word (ii, 11, 12; vi, 4, 18; ix, 5; xiv, 16; xvi, 6) it is of the rule of right, any constraining law of righteousness, as the laws of Wisdom cited above. Similarly "lawlessness" (ἀνομία v, 7, 23) and "lawless" ( ἄνομος, iv, 6; xv, 17; xvii, 2) indicate the absence of such a rule.

Part of this doctrine of created incorruption is the doctrine of the created nature of man. It is significant that the word "immortality" ( ἀθανασία) occurs only in this book out of all the Septuagint, except in 4 Maccabees (xiv, 5; xvi, 13) which, as will be shown hereafter, is a Stoic tract illustrated with examples from Jewish martyrology. Our author found the doctrine and the word in both Homer and Plato and it marks the attitude of the book and also the attitude of the new Judaism under Greek influence. In iii, 4, "their hope [i.e. the hope of the righteous] is full of immortality." In iv, 1, "in the memory of virtue is immortality," better than in children. In viii, 13, "through her [Wisdom] I [Solomon] shall have immortality," and in viii, 17, "and took thought in my heart that in kinship unto Wisdom is immortality." In xv, 3, "to know thy dominion (O God) is the root of immortality." In i, 15, "for righteousness is immortal" ( ἀθάνατος ). Four times only does "immortal" ( ἀθάνατος ) occur elsewhere in the Septuagint, thrice again in 4 Maccabees (vii, 3; xiv, 6; xviii, 23) and once in Ben Sira, xvii, 30, where it is denied, "because the son of man is not immortal." So man's "soul" is not the Hebrew néphesh but the Greek psyché, his ego, the first principle ( ἀρχή) of motion ( κινεῖν ), as in the Timaeus, 34 D. In xv, 11, there is a most singular paraphrase of Genesis ii, 7, describing the making of man in Greek technical and classical terms, "Because he knew not him that shaped him and breathed into him an active soul (ψυχὴν ἐνεργοῦσαν ) and inflated him with a life-giving spirit." Here "breathing in" is an Homeric expression, suggesting inspiring with courage and rage; the "active soul" suggests the Aristotelian "energy," physical and mental; the "inflated" is a Greek medical term, used already in the Septuagint; "the life-giving spirit" has association with Plato in the *Timaeus* and with Aristotle.

At the beginning of Book V of Plato's *Laws* (726) we read, "Of all a man's own belongings, the most divine ( θειότατον) is his soul, since it is most his own," and throughout the *Laws,* again and again, the secondary relation of the body (σῶμα) to the soul is stressed (870 B; 892 A; 896 C; 904 A; 959 B; 967 B). In the Book of Wisdom Solomon describes himself (viii, 19, 20) in very significant language as made of soul (ψυχή) and body (σῶμα). "Now I was of good natural disposition ( εὐφυής ) and I obtained [there fell to my lot; an Homeric usage] a good soul; nay, rather, being good, I came into a body undefiled." The term translated "of good natural disposition" is applied by Plato (*Republic,* 409 E) to both bodies and souls. The term "undefiled" ( ἀμίαντος ) is used twice elsewhere in the book (iii, 13; iv, 2) and never elsewhere in the Septuagint, except twice in 2 Maccabees, of the undefiled Temple. In all these passages the picture is of one who has come undefiled and triumphant through a long, hard conflict. The word is good, old Greek and is used by Plato in the *Laws* (777 E) of one who has proved himself undefiled by what is unholy or unjust.

The meaning of this passage seems to be: Man is body and soul, and both, to begin with, may be "good" ( ἀγαθος ) and undefiled (ἀμίαντος). Thus all matter is not necessarily evil; God's whole creation was good at the first, with no "death" in it. With good body and soul the child is of good natural disposition. The personality is the soul and comes into the body; so Solomon, a good personality, came into an undefiled body; that, it is implied, had been divinely arranged. In ii, 2a, the ungodly and foolish, on the other hand, are represented as saying that such things happen "by chance" ( αὐτοσχεδίως). This word does not occur elsewhere in the Septuagint and in the present usage it seems to go back to the Homeric "in close fight," "chance-medley." The body, as we have seen, is liable to corruption and the soul may be corrupted by the body. So ix, 15, "for a corruptible body is heavy on the soul, and the earthly tabernacle weighs down the mind full of cares." The vocabulary and ideas in this verse are Platonic throughout. The word for "tabernacle" ( σκῆνος ) is used here only in the Septuagint, but frequently in Plato for the tabernacle of the body. Our author probably avoided the kindred Septuagint word σκηνή because of its association with the theater just as Plato earlier had done. He uses, however, the normal word σκηνή in two places where it could not be avoided: in ix, 8, of "the holy tabernacle" in the wilderness and in xi, 2, of the tents of the Israelites. In the *Phaedo,* 81 C, five of the significant words here are used: body, heavy, earthy, soul, weigh down. The passage must have been in the mind of our author. The word translated here "full of cares" (πολυφροντίς) only occurs here in the Septuagint, and seldom elsewhere. It might be rendered "much thinking" and that fits the context better. A kindred word occurs in viii, 17, "taking thought (φροντίσας) in my heart."

We have already seen in vii, 27 that there are "holy souls" (ψυχαὶ ὅσιαι) into whom, from generation to generation, Wisdom passes and whom she makes friends of God and prophets. So God can be addressed (xi, 26) as "lover of souls." The Greek word here (φιλόψυχος) with its cognates, is used uniformly in classical Greek of one who loves his life and even holds to it in cowardice, and this, undoubtedly, is a daring application for a Greek audience. But the cases are different between a man holding onto his own "soul," or life, and God loving the souls of all His creatures. Almost certainly Ezekiel xvii, 4 was in the mind of our author, of course in its Septuagint form, "For all souls are mine ( ὅτι πᾶσαι αἱ ψυχαί ἐμαί εἰσιν); as the soul of the father, so also the soul of the son, they are mine; the soul that sins, this one (αὕτη) shall die." And then it goes on, that the righteous one shall surely live. So in i, 13, "For God made not death"—the reiterated doctrine of this book—"neither delighteth he when the living perish." And in i, 6, the other part is given: "For Wisdom is a spirit that loveth man" (πνεῦμα φιλάνθρωπον); in vii, 23, Wisdom is again "a lover of man" and "a lover of good" ( φιλάγαθος ). In xii, 19 it is the righteous ( δίκαιος ) who, taught by God, must be a lover of men. It is worthy of notice that such Greek compounds in φιλ- hardly occur in the parts of the Septuagint translated from the Hebrew Old Testament, but are common in the Apocrypha and especially in this book. The point will return in dealing with the Hebrew "colonizing" of Palestine.

It is time now to turn to a consideration of Wisdom, for Wisdom is really the heroine of this book. The book is a reconstruction of the spiritual and temporal history of Israel round two ideas: first that the divine Wisdom, as a personality, was the guiding and controlling power in that history and, second, that the transfer of Israel from Egypt to Palestine and its settlement there should be regarded as the sending out of a colony, after the Greek fashion, and its settlement in previously foreign territory. For our author Egypt belonged to the Greek world; he takes that for granted. He himself speaks, reads and writes Greek and feels himself part of that world. The native Egyptians of the old stock are in another class entirely. They and their religion are absurd, repulsive and un-Greek, as much as they are un-Hebrew. It was with them that the Hebrews had trouble in the old days when Jehovah rescued His people with a high hand and sent them forth. That sending forth is represented anachronistically as like the sending out of a Greek colony as though the Greek world had then been in Egypt and the Jews had been part of it. And Jehovah in this and in everything works through a person called Wisdom. She was "the artificer of all things" (vii, 22; xiv, 2), but she, though she was from the beginning of creation, had come into being—i.e. was not from all eternity; her very nature belonged to mystery (vi, 22). In her there is spirit and she is a breath ( ἀτμίς ) of the power ( δυνάμις ) of God; so she is all powerful ( παντοδύναμος ) like God Himself and may even be called Power itself (i, 3). So the author labors to obliterate in the minds of his Greek friends all idea that the Hebrews were a race, strange, hostile, inhuman and uncivilized, enemies to all other peoples. They were apart in that they had received divine guidance from the very beginning, but that guidance had been the very Wisdom and divine Reason that the Greek philosophers had tried to find and follow. There is nothing in the book, as we have already seen, about a law of prescripts and ritual designed to put a barrier between the Jews and all other nations, but there is much in it as to the rule of righteousness and the guidance of Wisdom and the kindness and love of God. Men, guided by Wisdom, can become the friends of God. And when judgment comes it is the Greek Justice ( Δίκη ) that brings it (i, 8; xiv, 31; xviii, 11); in the two first of these passages Justice is personified exactly as in Greek usage. There is no reference from beginning to end to the Fear of Jehovah.

In the Book of Proverbs, which our author certainly knew, that Fear is reiterated and also in Ben Sira and Ecclesiastes, which he may have known. But in his book there is no slightest reference to it and that must be of intention. In the plagues which came upon the Egyptians (chapters xvi *ff.*) their fear is vividly expressed but that is panic terror and different from that godly fear meant in the phrase, the Fear of Jehovah. Further, our author says explicitly (xvii, 12) that "fear is nothing but a betrayal of the aids which come from reasoning" ( λογισμός ). The Fear of Jehovah, therefore, could never be for him the basis for a rational life, and this remark seems intended as a tacit, or implied, rejection of that position frequently expressed in the Old Testament.

We have already considered in Chapter iv a doctrine which grew up among Palestinian Hebrews that there is a personified Reason, coeternal with Jehovah Himself. That doctrine as to coeternity was carefully expunged, as we have seen, by the Greek translator of Proverbs viii; other dangerous passages in the Book of Proverbs were also removed or changed in the Greek version. The conception, however, of Reason, or, in the Greek, Wisdom ( σοφία ), as a personality had remained. Enough, too, had reached our author in his Greek Bible to show that the beginning or source of Wisdom had been a much debated question. The position that that beginning was the Fear of the Lord he, as we have seen, definitely rejected. However many passages stood in his Greek Bible asserting that, he would have none of them. Ben Sira's reiteration of this in his book, if our author had read it, must have irritated him, and he may have explicitly set himself in contradiction. "All Wisdom is the Fear of the Lord" (xix, 20); "the end of the Fear of the Lord is Wisdom" (xxi, 11); "there is nothing better than the Fear of the Lord" (xxiii, 27)—such sayings were irrational to him. Fear to him, as we have seen, was essentially irrational and a thing to be got rid of. In this he was accepting the universally held Greek position: by the practising of courage from youth up frights and fears were to be conquered (e.g. Plato, *Laws, 791*). The drastic saying in Proverbs iv, 7, "The beginning of Reason [or Wisdom] is Get Reason" had been dropped from his Bible, or it might have attracted him. But one word occurs there again and again (twenty-one times) and fixed his attention. It is used as a translation for the Hebrew word meaning "discipline," the discipline for life of the young. But this word, παιδεία, meant, rather, for him and perhaps still more for his Greek readers, "training" and "teaching," broadly "education"; such is its normal classical use. How he himself felt as to its meaning we cannot be sure. It may be that his Jewish-Greek circle in Alexandria held more closely to the idea "discipline." But he was writing for heathen Greek readers and handles it as they would understand it. Inasmuch, then, as it is used so normally in Greek, he built up from it, in his celebrated Sorites, his answer to the question as to the beginning of Wisdom: This Sorites, or logical chain, comes vi, 17-19: "For her [Wisdom's] truest beginning is desire of education; and thinking of education is love of her; and love of her is keeping of her laws; and attention to her laws is a guaranteeing of incorruption, and incorruption works being near to God. So desire of Wisdom leads to kingship." Therefore—Solomon drives home his point to his colleagues, the kings and judges of the earth—if you rejoice in your royal rule, honor Wisdom that it may continue.

It will be noticed that Wisdom's *truest* ( ἀληθεστάτη ) beginning is the desire of this training or education. We have here an evident allusion to the dispute on that point; our author regards this as the truest of all the assertions; but he plainly rejected absolutely that which began Wisdom from the fear of the Lord. And it will be noticed, too, how this training of the personality, which is essentially desire of Wisdom, means "incorruption," that fundamental idea in the book, by which the original, divinely given, state of the universe, is maintained.

But what is this Wisdom and in what respects does she differ either from the Reason of the eighth chapter of Proverbs or from the Wisdom admitted by Ben Sira? Solomon, addressing the Judges of the Earth, leads up to her at once, but he leads off from the Lord Himself. He calls upon them to love "righteousness" (δικαιοσύνη ) and to think ( φρονήσατε ) of the Lord in "goodness" and seek Him in simplicity of heart. This is a curious compound of Greek philosophical language and Old Testament piety. "Righteousness" and "thought" are two of the four cardinal virtues of Greek philosophy; all four of them are given in viii, 7, these two with "rational temperance" ( σωφροσύνη ) and "courage" ( ἀνδρεία ) ; see, for example, Plato's *Laws* 631 C. For "goodness" (ἀγαθότης) Plato would have preferred another word ἀρετή "virtue," which our author does use iv, 1 ; v, 13 ; viii, 7. The word used by our author here might have sounded rather broad and general for a Greek. The phrase "in simplicity of heart" comes verbally from David's prayer, 1 Chronicles xxix, 17, at the consecration of Solomon as king. To find the Lord they must not apply tests to Him ( πειράζω, again an Homeric word) ; He is seen clearly by those who do not distrust Him. For crooked reasonings separate from Him, but the real Power in the world, when tried out, confutes the unthinking.

So Wisdom is reached, for it is she who is meant by this tested and confuting Power. The obscure and allusive way in which the word is used may be due in part to a certain exasperating "preciousness" in the style of the author, but it is also possible that "the Power," already in Alexandrine thinking, was a known expression for the manifestation and working of God in the world. The word occurs twelve times in this book. Philo, later, carried the usage much further and the word occurs often in the Hermetic writings. The statement as to Wisdom goes on: that she "will not enter into a soul using evil arts ( κακότεχνος ) nor dwell in a body pledged to sin, for the Holy Spirit of training [cf. "thy Holy Spirit" used of Wisdom, ix, 17] will flee deceit ( δόλος ) and arise and go away from stupid reasonings, and will feel shamed [ ἐλεγχθήσεται, an Homeric usage] when unrighteousness comes in, for Wisdom is a humane spirit." In the two words "deceit" and "using evil arts" used here in close context, there is an allusion to *Iliad* xv, 14, where a charge in exactly these terms is brought against Hera.

Another description of Wisdom (vii, 21-27) is equally significant. Solomon, as always, is the speaker: "All things secret and manifest I knew, for Wisdom, the Artificer of all things, taught me. For there is in her a Spirit which is intellectual, holy; sole of her kind, manifold, subtle [ ?sensitive?] ; easily moving, piercing, undefiled [ ?undefiling?] ; clear, harmless, loving goodness, keen; unhindered, beneficent, humane; trusty, secure, care-free; all-powerful, all-surveying; spreading through all spirits that are intellectual, pure and most subtle [?sensitive?]. For Wisdom is more moving than any motion and pervades and spreads through all things by her purity. For she is a vapor (rising) from the Power of God and an unmixed streaming forth of the Glory of the Almighty; therefore, nothing polluted can steal into her. For she is a radiant reflection of Eternal Light and an unstained mirror of the working of God and an image of His goodness. Being one she can do all things and remaining in herself she makes new all things."

Here the combination of Greek philosophy and Hebrew piety is very plain; the philosophical terms are used to make the piety attractive and intelligible to the Greek mind. The description begins and ends with "all things"; Wisdom expresses a complete philosophy of life. She is intellect and also holiness; the Artificer of all, like God Himself. The word used, τεχνῖτις, in this sense is apparently to avoid δημιουργός, skilled workman, which had unfortunate associations. Wisdom, that is, is not the Demiurge of the *Timaeus*. She is a spirit (πνεῦμα) and spreads through all pure, intellectual spirits. This again is the Stoic theory of the universal immanence of the divine πνεῦμα. She is all-powerful like God Himself and also a vapor (ἀτμίς, vapor or steam thrown off by heat; in the Septuagint of smoke of burning incense or any burning) rising from His Power. This is a very singular expression and must have had some origin. It is somewhat like Ben Sira's "mist" (ὁμίχλη) which came out from the mouth of the Most High and covered the earth (Ecclesiasticus, xxiv, 3). Ben Sira's descriptive language in his use of this word, and throughout, can be linked up, point by point, with Hebrew usage, and it, in turn, certainly could have suggested our author's "vapor" or "smoke." The Greek translator of Ben Sira, however, uses ἀτμίς four times of incense or furnace smoke (xxii, 24; xxiv, 15; xxxviii, 28; xliii, 4) and one of these is in Wisdom's Praise of herself (xxiv, 1-22). There (verse 15 of the English version, 21 of the Greek) she describes how part of her ministry before the Lord was "as the fume (ἀτμίς) of frankincense in the tabernacle." If this connection is sound, and it seems very direct, it means that the Book of Wisdom was written after 132 B.C., the date given in the Prologue to Ecclesiasticus. But Ben Sira's imagery in describing Wisdom in this passage is Hebrew and here the wording and picture are Greek. The verbs "spread through" and "pervade" (διήκειν, χωρεῖν) are used by Stoic writers to express how God, who is also Reason (νοῦς, λόγος) and Fate, pervades the world (Diogenes Laertius, vii, 134 ff., 147 ff.; these sections have much of the vocabulary of this description). "More moving than any motion" suggests, also, the Stoic use of "the moving things" for "the desirable things"; there may be a play on that here. The word for "streaming out" (ἀπόρροια) was used by Plato (Phaedrus, 251 B) for the effluence of beauty which enters through the eyes and by Empedocles for the means by which outward things make themselves perceptible to the mind. The figure of Wisdom as the image ( εἰκών ) of the goodness of God goes back to the last paragraph of the Timaeus where the Cosmos is "a perceptible God made in the image of the Intelligible, most great and good and fair and perfect in its generation . . . even this one, sole of its kind." The vocabulary here is the vocabulary of our author, although his Wisdom is certainly not the visible Cosmos of Plato. Yet she, too, is "one" and "sole of her kind" (μονογενής). The word in this description which is most alien to classical Greek is "Glory" ( δόξα ). In classical Greek it could mean "reputation" and even "honor," but hardly the Glory of God. But in contemporary Alexandrine usage there must have been some basis for its application by the Septuagint translators to render thirty-four expressions in Hebrew of the divine glory. It may be well, also, to note that there is no trace in this book of the Stoic use of Logos for the Reason of the world, the active principle—that is God—which pervades the material principle, ἡ ὕλη. Logos in this book is always "speech," except ii, 2, where it is human reason, explained by the ungodly ( ἀσεβεῖς ) as a spark produced by the motion of the heart; these seem to have been Stoics (Diogenes Laertius, vii, 156). In xviii, 22 Logos is human speech in prayer, and in ix, 1, xii, 9, xvi, 12, xviii, 15 it is divine speech, the utterance not the mind of God. In ix, 1, 2 there is a clear distinction between God's *word* by which He made all things and His Wisdom by which He equipped man for his rule of the world in holiness and righteousness. This Wisdom sits beside God on His throne. But the author twice uses the word "matter" (ὕλη), once for the formless matter (the precise Greek philosophical term) out of which

God shaped the world (xi, 17) and once for the earthy matter out of which a potter makes brittle vessels (xv, 13). These are the only occurrences of the word in this sense in the Septuagint. Elsewhere it is used four times for "wood" and once for the materials used in a book.

But what, more particularly, is the relation of this Wisdom to men and to God? We have seen that she sits beside Him, as "assessor" ( πάρεδρος ) on His throne. So Themis, Justice personified, is the assessor of Zeus in Pindar (*Olym.* viii, 22); our author may have been thinking of this very passage. The problem of the nature of Wisdom and of her relation to God was one of the mysteries of his time. She was created, but was from the beginning of creation (vi, 22); similarly she is the beginning ( γένεσις ) of all good things and comes leading them (vii, 12). God gives her to whom He pleases. He gave her to Solomon on Solomon's prayer to Him (vii, 7; viii, 21). Yet in vi, 12-14, men seek her directly and she is found of them; if anyone seeks her diligently he will find her sitting at his gates; here again she is πάρεδρος. She is the guide of men; yet God guides even her (vii, 15). In Proverbs viii, even in the Septuagint translation, Wisdom goes out herself in search of men and summons them to her; she works independently of God. But our author labors to preserve the supremacy and primacy of God, while using the conception of Wisdom as His agent with men bringing them to Him.

Again, our author introduces a singular difference between his Wisdom and the Wisdom of whom he had read in his Book of Proverbs and whom he had found described, if the above combination is sound, in the Book of Ben Sira. In the Greek Proverbs (viii, 32; ix, 12) it is her son that Wisdom addresses and the attitude is maternal—or paternal—throughout. In Ben Sira the same thing holds. In his book, iv, 11, Wisdom exalts her sons and that is the general attitude; Wisdom personified is a continuation of family discipline. But one passage is different and curious. In xv, 2, "as a mother shall she [Wisdom] meet him and receive him as a wife, married in her virginity" ( γυνὴ παρθενίας ). This probably means nothing more than "a young woman," and that is the exact meaning of the Hebrew text that has reached us. But what Ben Sira meant by this it is almost impossible to guess, except that

Wisdom would be devoted to him. We have already seen how marked an anti-feminist he was; he knew that there were good wives, but he held that the man was very fortunate who had found one. In general a wife was a necessary evil; he could never forget that by a woman (Eve) came death and the beginning of sin (xxv, 24).

With this origin of death and sin and also as to the whole essential structure of the world our author, as we have seen, completely disagreed. And his personal attitude towards the personified Wisdom was equally different. Whether moved by his Greek training, or in consideration of his Greek readers, he transformed this spiritual guidance into something more akin to Greek ideas. He dropped the picture of Wisdom as a guiding and training Mother and put in its place the ever attractive Greek fancy of an inspiring nymph. He could do that because the word νύμφη meant also "bride" and he could portray Solomon as seeking Wisdom as his wife. Yet it is to be remembered that the use of the word in the Septuagint is ambiguous. It means "daughter-in-law" as often as "bride" and he could have found other unambiguous words if the idea "wife" alone had been in his mind, e.g. γυνή or, more warmly, ἡ πλησίον, often in the Song of Songs. But the word nymph which he chose had another and a most suggestive meaning. He uses the word γυνή once only, iii, 12, speaking of foolish wives. The nymphs, on the other hand, were "feminine personifications of elemental life," "brides of nature," "ideal but akin to our humanity" (L. R. Farnell in Hastings' *Dictionary of Religion,* ix, 226). Poets and philosophers could dream of them and seek their help. They were part of the very deepest associations of life. Calypso herself, "the beautiful and dread goddess," is repeatedly called a nymph. When Odysseus at last reaches his native land, his first worship is addressed to the nymphs in the cave sacred to them, where he had been wont to offer sacrifice to them, and these nymphs he now hailed with loving prayers (*Odyssey,* xiii, 347 *ff.*). When Plato makes Socrates talk to Phaedrus about love, in the plane tree shade, on the grass, by the Ilissus, Socrates finds the place filled with a divine presence and he himself, as it were, taken by the nymphs—nympholept, and swept along in frenzy in his speech (*Phaedrus,* 238 D). Thus in the nymphs the supernatural came

closely and easily to men. But their influence could be still more
spiritually educative. When Plutarch (*Moralia,* "On Roman Fortune," viii) tells the story of Numa and Egeria—a story which he
is careful to say, he does not believe—Egeria is a nymph, one of
the dryads, "a wise goddess," δαίμονα σοφήν, and has become the
bride of Numa and his guide and teacher. As such a nymph-bride
Solomon sought for Wisdom from God. "Her I loved,"—it is
Solomon speaking, viii, 2 *ff.*—"and sought out from my youth and
I sought to take her for myself as bride ( νύμφη) and I fell in love
with her beauty. She glorifies her noble nature ( εὐγένεια ) having
life together with God ( συμβίωσις) and the Maker of all things
loved her; for she is an initiate ( μύστις ) of the knowledge of God
and a chooser of his works. . . . I determined, then, to take her, to
have life together with her" (πρὸς συμβίωσιν, as she with God).
This he did, knowing that he would find in her counsel and encour-
agement and honor amongst men. He would be guided in his judging and governing. "When I have come into my house I shall find
rest beside her [my wife], for intercourse with her has no bitter-
ness nor life with her pain, but gladness and joy. . . . For in her
kinship ( συγγένεια ) is immortality and in her affection full
delight . . . and in the exercise of intercourse with her is understanding." The words here are carefully chosen for their double
suggestion of the bride and the counsellor. Then Solomon turns to
God and prays Him to give him Wisdom. She who sits beside Him
on His throne, who knows His works and was present when He
was making the world, to send her forth out of the holy heavens
and from the throne of His glory to bid her come. Only as God
sends His holy spirit and gives Wisdom are men taught and saved.

So when a Greek reader came to this nymph, whom Solomon
had sought and found as his bride, he recognized at once such an
idea as he already knew. It was just such a case as Numa and his
Egeria with one enormous difference. Solomon's Egeria was in
closest kinship with all the operations and structure of nature and
had known all that from its beginning; she belonged to nature like
the Greek nymphs. We may compare the picture of Reason in
Proverbs as the voice of theology speaking in and through nature;
see Chapter IV above. But she belonged also to God, that tremendous Lord of all; she was His Wisdom and was sent by Him to the

particular men whom He chose. So through this conception of their own, full of such attractive beauty, the Greek reader could be led to that of the one Jehovah, the Maker and Ruler of all and to the conception of an eternal Righteousness and immortal life through and in Him. It will be noticed, too, with what delicacy this relationship is handled, and how great is the contrast with Philo's God having intercourse with Knowledge and thus begetting the creation. It is very easy for such metaphors to run wild. Again it is to be observed that our author never uses allegory as Philo does. Philo really annuls the historic event; the allegory that for him lies in it is his fact. But in this book the events stand firm, and we see the causes behind them, and we can draw from them spiritual meanings. The history of the Hebrew people was real but it was also spiritual, for it showed God working behind and in it. Another distinction is worth drawing. Clement of Alexandria in his *Exhortation to the Greeks* attacks the personal lives of the Greek gods and the nymphs he would have reckoned with the demigods ( ἡμίθεοι ), a secondary rank of divinities, whom he denounces at the end of his second chapter. See, too, precise mention of the nymphs, Chapter IV, p. 132, in Butterworth's edition in the Loeb Library. Our author ignores the personal Greek gods, as the educated Greeks of his time did. He attacks the absurdities of the Egyptian gods, but that was the attitude of all educated Greeks. Clement, also, attacks in detail and in the same spirit the Mysteries; our author follows Plato's attitude, and attacks the obscene rites of the Canaanites, but he leaves the Greek rites untouched. The Egyptians and the Canaanites were his enemies and not the Greeks. Again Clement specifically forbids the practice of the art of sculpture (pp. 132, 140, in the Loeb edition) ; it is dangerous and the Scriptures forbid it. But for our author God is the first author of beauty (xiii, 3) and he denounces only the image that is worshiped as a god. His attitude was thus a mixture of Platonism and Hebrew monotheism; but the Platonism was there. Through it he could make attractive to the Greek mind the Hebrew fundamental conceptions. Yet another point shows the same consideration of his Greek audience. Ben Sira has no doctrine of immortality; for him "the covenant from the beginning is, Thou shalt die the death" (xiv, 17). But for our author God made not death (i, 13) ; death is an invasion of the primal incorruption; the processes of the world—the Lord's world—are essentially healthy. And after death the continued existence of all, good and bad, is accepted. But there is no picture of how and where they exist. When the word Hades occurs it is either Death (i, 14; ii, 1) or the vague realm of Hades as a Greek might have spoken of it (xvi, 13; xvii, 14). But our author in the last passage is careful to add "powerless" ( $\dot{a}\delta\acute{v}a\tau o s$ ) to both Hades and Night. The souls of the righteous are in the hand of God (iii, 1); they are in peace as they lived in hope (iii, 3, 4) and they rest (iv, 7). There is no slightest touch of the Hebrew Sheol; everything is spiritualized; there is no judgment scene. The verses telling how "the righteous"—not the Jews— "in the time of their visitation" shall shine out, judge and have dominion and the Lord shall reign over them (iii, 7, 8) are vague of evident purpose. This is not a triumph of the people of Israel over the heathen nations which have oppressed them, as in the Apocalypses; it is the triumph of righteousness. Our author did not wish to use the current Jewish pictures and still less could he use such Greek mythology and pictures from the Orphic mysteries as are given in the *Phaedo*, 107 C-114 E, but his ideas are essentially Platonic and would reach the heart of any thoughtful and educated Greek. They may easily have been quite distasteful to his fellow Jews.

The second Greek idea which has influenced the structure of the book is that of the colony, $\dot{a}\pi o\iota\kappa\acute{\iota}a$. The sending of a colony in the Greek states was a means of relieving pressure of population at home and of spreading the Greek civilization abroad. A colony was sent out, very often at the suggestion and under the guidance of one of the Oracles, to occupy non-Greek territory. The same word $\dot{a}\pi o\iota\kappa\acute{\iota}a$ is used quite often in the Septuagint but always of an entirely different thing, the forcible Exile or Captivity of the Jews. In the Book of Wisdom, however, it is used in the Greek sense and presents Israel to Greek readers as having been sent out from Egypt under divine guidance to colonize Palestine. As the Oracles used to send out Greek colonies, so Jehovah had sent His people. The latter part of the book is taken up with the description of the sending of this colony to Palestine and the settling of it there. That is why the book ends where it does and does not go on through the later history of Israel in Palestine. The colony had been founded. To the Greek reader it must have been like one of the stories in Herodotus of such sendings of colonies, with Jehovah playing the part of the Oracle.

In xii, 3 *ff.* we are told how the old inhabitants of Palestine practised detestable works and unholy rites and that it was God's counsel to destroy them at the hands of the fathers of Israel that that most precious land might receive a worthy colony ( ἀποικία ) of God's children. Here the word is used in the Greek sense, as nowhere else in the Septuagint. In xviii, 3 there is another allusion, which may be exactly translated, "Instead of which thou [God] didst provide a burning pillar of fire, a guide in an unknown journey and an unharming sun in an ambitious foreign service." The English version, "for their proud exile," does not recognize either the meaning of the Greek words or the purpose of the author in using them here. The noun "ambition" ( φιλοτιμία ) occurs already of an artist in xiv, 18, its only occurrence in the Septuagint, and the cognate φιλότιμος, "ambitious," occurs only here and in 3 Maccabees. "Foreign service" ( ξενιτεία ) occurs here only in the Septuagint, but is good classical Greek in that meaning. Our author could not have expressed his parallel more clearly. As for the Pillar of Fire and the "unharming" (ἀβλαβῆ) sun, it is very plain that our author in all his narrative of the Exodus and the Desert wanderings went beyond what he read in his Greek Bible and drew freely on legends which we now, in part, can read in the Targums and Philo. Thus Philo says of the Pillar of Cloud, which guided the Israelites in the daytime, that it had a light as of the sun. But our author says that that sun was unharming and not like the deadly oriental sun that Greek colonies had often to endure. Plato uses the word ἀβλαβής of harmless pleasures and, in the *Laws*, 953 A, of strangers admitted to sojourn for a time in his ideal state.

From all the above it will be plain that our author was an open-minded Jew living in an educated Greek environment which had deeply affected him. He held fixedly to such fundamentals as the unity and the spiritual personality of Jehovah and His immediate government of the world; that that government was righteous and that righteousness thus was immortal; that the structure of the world made for health and life; that in the world there was a created Being, Wisdom, a personality like God Himself, who had existed since the first creation; that this Being was the personal guide of men of good will in their lives. He held also that God had revealed Himself, His will and His character, to all men in His creation but had done so more directly and explicitly to the Hebrew people. He had done that through His holy spirit, this Wisdom, sent down to men (ix, 17); even as she had guarded to the end the Father of the human race, delivered him from his transgressions, and taught him to rule the world (x, 1, 2), so she had worked, guiding and delivering, through the history of the Hebrew race (x, xi). That race was the great example of the immediate guidance of God. But this was not to make them proud and overbearing —a dominant race in the world—but that they and all men might learn that righteousness was good and that the righteous must be a lover of men (xii, 19). Mercy on all men; love of all things that are; preserving and sparing of all "for they are thine, O Sovereign Lord, Lover of souls!" (xi, 26). The message of Israel, for our author, is in the Hundredth Psalm, "All people that on earth do dwell. . . . He made us and we are His"—although his Greek Bible did not so read. Thus the particularity and the peculiarity of Israel have vanished; their message is for all the human race. Naturally, then, when our author speaks of the Law he means the universal law of righteousness and not the Mosaic ritual and statutes. He shows no sign of caring in the least for these. As Paul went out preaching Christ and Christ only, so he would preach to the Greek world this Holy Spirit of Jehovah, Wisdom herself. And through that Wisdom which they all knew he would illumine to them what was the essential in the faith of Jews.

But it is also plain that in his time there was much prejudice against the Jews. Behind the book is the eternally afflicted Jew holding to his righteousness against the contempt of the world. He is living in a murmuring generation in which there is much talking against ideas of God and goodness and immortality (i, 7-11). Especially violent are Epicureans—although they are not named as such—evidently of the baser sort, whose motto is not only, Let us eat and drink for tomorrow we die, but whose attitude is directly hostile to those who hold to their righteousness. "Let us

oppress the righteous poor . . . let our strength be a law of righteousness . . . that which is weak is found to be of no service . . .
let us lie in wait for the righteous man, because he is of disservice
to us . . . and upbraideth us and layeth to our charge sins. . . . He
professeth to have knowledge of God . . . he is grievous to us . . .
because his life is unlike other men's" (ii, 10-15). So the righteous
are tested in this world but their souls are in the hand of God and
they are in peace (iii, 1-3). God will remember them, visit them
and restore them (iii, 4-9). This is a restoration of the divine rule
and kingdom on earth; but it is not Israel that is to rule the world
but divine wisdom and righteousness which are in the very structure
of the world (v, 17, 20) and which will overcome foolishness and
wickedness.

There follows (iii, 10 ff.) a very singular and difficult passage.
The wicked, apparently, held up against the righteous their own
many children and length of days, while the righteous often were
childless and died young. "But happy is the barren who is undefiled; happy the eunuch who has wrought no lawless deed." "Better
is childlessness with virtue, for in the memory of virtue is immortality." The Jews in Egypt, apparently, were tempted away from
their faith and its righteousness to marry with the heathen. This
is adultery for our author and he stands against it (iii, 16). Better
even not to marry at all and to have no children, than to have children from such unions (iv, 3, 4). This does not seem to be a doctrine of asceticism, but a reflection of an actual situation, and the
pressure of that situation has forced our author to a position of
antagonism against the Hebrew idea of the blessing that is in
children and against the rejection of the eunuch in Hebrew law
from the sanctuary (iii, 14). It has been observed (e.g. Lane's
*Modern Egyptians,* Chapter vi) that foreign women residing in
Egypt are often childless and that children of foreigners, born in
Egypt, seldom live to a mature age. Apparently a Jewish family
resident in Egypt would die out unless it completely crossed itself
with native stocks and to that our author could not bring himself.
It is curious that in the *Hermetica,* which were written in Egypt at
the beginning of the third century A.D., there is a similar problem of
childlessness and a description of the unhappy fate of the souls of

the childless after death (*Hermetica,* Lib. ii, end). To be childless is not only a great misfortune but also a great sin.

It does not seem necessary to pursue further ·the proof how great and evident was the effect on Jewish thought when it actually came into contact with Greek philosophy. The contrast between Ecclesiastes and Ecclesiasticus on the one hand, and the Book of Wisdom on the other is complete. The thinking of Ben Sira and of Ecclesiastes can be explained throughout as a legitimate development of old Hebrew ideas and thought; the thinking of the author of *Wisdom* is soaked, words and ideas, in Greek. Even the maternal Reason of the old Hebrews is transformed into a Greek nymph, beautiful and wise. If any further proof is needed let the first three chapters of 4 Maccabees be read, where a Stoic tractate on the rule of the passions by reason introduces the horrible account of the martyrdom of Eleazar and the Seven Brethren with their Mother. This is an utterly different example from that in the Book of Wisdom, for in 4 Maccabees Greek philosophy is woven through a picture of the most intense Jewish nationalism. It is noteworthy that it is only in this Fourth Book of Maccabees in all the Septuagint that the words φιλοσοφεῖν, φιλοσοφία, φιλόσοφος occur, with the single exception of φιλόσοφος in the Septuagint translation of Daniel i, 20. And we have seen, again and again above, how close the vocabulary of the Books of Maccabees often is to that of this Book of Wisdom.

There have been some references above to the Hermetic tractates written in Egypt about three centuries later than our Book of Wisdom. There are things in those tractates which sound like echoes, but they seem to come from a common *religious* background, an emotional attitude to the divine behind life, rather than from any theological or philosophical schemes, certainly not from any organized synagogue or church. Many things had made their imprint on the Hermetists: the fundamental Platonic religious ideas, God and the Good, the Cosmos between God and man; there is a plain attempt to spiritualize the Creation in Genesis (Lib. i), and to adopt the Christian conception of a new birth by the will ( θέλημα ) of God (Lib. xiii). Theological dogmas and philosophical abstractions fall away and the human soul is naked and yearning towards God. But this is not Jehovah. It is far more the Platonic Divine (τὸ θεῖον), made personal and individual. All the theologies have melted together into this yearning; all the mythologies have left their imprint in one image or another. The temper of mind and the religious attitude of our author were much the same and he, too, may have made his imprint with his doctrine of a Wisdom who brings men to God and of God as eternal Good and Righteousness.

# CHAPTER VII

## PLATO'S "LAWS"—ECCLESIASTES—BEN SIRA

SEVERAL times it has been suggested above that the philosophical genius of the Hebrews was Platonic in type rather than Aristotelian. This appears especially in the dominant position which it allows to the idea as distinguished from the observed, or, at least, observable fact. What we would call facts did not matter to the Hebrews when they were following a clear and, for them subjectively, certain idea. The idea was their reality and prevented them, in general, seeing the discordant facts of life. Those of them who did see the facts were in revolt against the whole Hebrew scheme and had to find a new standing-ground for themselves. This, as has been shown above, they did in various ways. But even while dissenting in all these ways they retained the idea of a single personality behind life and in ultimate control of life. They differed only in their description of this personality.

About 190 B.C. there were, as we have seen, two Hebrew writers who differed upon this point about as widely as at all possible. Ben Sira, the author of the book which we call Ecclesiasticus, and a man whom we may call for convenience Ecclesiastes as he was the author of the book commonly called by that name, practically agreed only in accepting the fact that there was a personality thus behind life; on the nature of this personality they differed absolutely.

About a century and a half earlier, Plato had died (the traditional date is 347 B.C.) and left as his last work an elaborate book, *The Laws,* which stands in the most remarkable contrast with his earlier writings and especially with *The Republic.* Devout Platonists have had no great liking for the book as it shows the Master as a disillusioned, almost disappointed, old man, turning from the free speculation of his earlier days to seek a secure resting-place in the old Greek institutions and usages—religious, social, political— and on the basis of these to build up a partially ideal, but still practical, and practicable, state. The mark of age is strong upon the book. In it old institutions and old men are handled with reverence and the arrogance and impetuosity of youth are severely checked. The young must not censure laws but praise them; throughout, the pedagogical principle is followed that if you are not allowed to say something, in time you will not wish to say it; the old may censure cautiously before magistrates or among those of their own age but never to the young (634 D E). According to Plato's mind the training of the people was everything and formed the most important part of the administration of a state. So, throughout this book, his ideas are ruled by pedagogic considerations, much as in the Book of Proverbs. "Bring up a child in the way he should go and when he is old he will not depart from it" runs through his thought. But the people, for him, never pass beyond the pupillary status; they are always under teachers and controllers, administrators of a fixed system. Even the Nocturnal Council is under the constitution and under the gods. So the people never reaches the point of education when it can be set free and have its destinies in its own hands. Sparta has more influence on this ideal constitution than Athens. And still nearer is the benevolent tutelage which the Jesuits achieved for a century and a half (1608-1767) at Paraguay —"a delightful nursery, an innocent Paradise." Political power is concentrated in the hands of the old and the resultant state, it has been said, would be likely to strike the youth of our day as a Paradise for the old but a Purgatory for the young (Bury, i, p. XV). Apparently the Greek world of that day was passing through a phase of constitution-making and had some faith in the application of philosophy to existent institutions. This was Plato's contribution.

But this Plato is very far from the disciple of Socrates who had, in his youth, ridden out so gallantly on free intellectual adventure. The morning wind of that dawn of the world's thinking has blown by, and Plato has lapsed back into the rut of the traditional possibilities and inheritances of the Greek scheme, out of which Socrates had shaken him. It is true that he retains his devotion to the soul, the Psyche, and makes it the basis of the hope of mankind, the link between man and the gods. It is prior to the body and should rule the body and the fact of the existence of the soul is practically his proof of the existence of the whole spiritual life, a proof worked out in a curiously mechanistic fashion. Only a thing "alive" (ἔμψυχον), i.e. possessing "soul" (ψυχή), can originate motion; motions of the soul lie behind purely mechanical motions; therefore soul must precede body and nature cannot be explained in terms of mechanism (896 ff.). Yet when the scheme itself of this ideal state is made plain one cannot help wondering how far any-one's soul could develop in it. The life in that carefully isolated state is practically one of farming enlivened, if the word can be used, with the most strictly supervised and traditional gymnastic, dancing and singing. Freedom of thought and action are restricted to the utmost possible degree; for the young the freedom is to agree with the state. So we have the world of an old man's dream, a tired old man, sick of the infinite, distracting possibilities in life, with their haunting risks, and hoping and scheming for security above all else. The courage to face the future for which we would look in a disciple of Socrates is all gone. Even the impossible ideal-ism of the communistic state in the *Republic* is gone. He continues to hold that such a state, in which every member in all his activities, physical and mental, was completely merged in the one body of the state, is still the absolute ideal (739 B C D). But this state of his old age, which he is working out, is the only practicable one, if indeed even it be practicable. It is the old Greek ideals and forms of thought and living which have come back to him. The gods, daemons and heroes have to be conserved, although behind them and embracing them there is "god" ( ὁ θεός ) and even God ( θεός as a proper name), "a certain God" ( θεός τις, 691 D), and Zeus on the border line between being an Olympian and God as a unique individual. The gods are good with all goodness and careful of the whole (900 D). Thus Plato was sure of a divine background to life, whatever was to be its name, and sure, too, that in some form, even polytheistic or polydaemonistic, that background must be the basis of all ordered life in the world. All mortal creatures are pos-sessions of the gods (902 B). From the minor deities of state, of shrine, of family, man must begin to build up his life (717).

To us, with our strongly monistic tendencies, this apparent indif-ference to the question whether there is one God or many is very difficult. It takes us back into the state of mind from which the Hebrews emerged when they completely turned their backs on the polytheistic Semitic scheme of the Unseen World and changed their Elohím from a plural to a singular, though keeping the plural form, and that singular a heavily marked personality with a proper name, Jehovah. The plural had indicated the complex of the inhabitants of the spirit world; the singular swept that away and, at most, left with Jehovah a scheme of "messengers" and "spirits" who had no personality in themselves. Plato, and the Greeks generally, seem to have felt no need of such a simplification of the divine background to life. Yet what simplification there is in the Platonic conception points to a theism as precise as that of the Hebrews and not to any all-embracing and all-effacing pantheism. For there are many "souls" in existence, good and bad, as in the world there is order and disorder; but the movements in the heavens are orderly and show the working of the perfectly good supreme soul who is "our King" (ἡμῶν ὁ βασιλεύς, 904 A). That the Greeks, thus, had no feeling towards unity is our greatest difficulty in entering into their theological mind. In their philosophical mind the way was clear, as here with Plato, and a single step only was needed in their theology. But the pressure in Plato's mind towards unity was not sufficiently strong and he evidently preferred as a practical basis, on which men could meet, to keep the multiplicity of the Greek scheme.

From this came one very important consequence. It was practically impossible for a Greek to have the emotional relationship to God which was so marked a characteristic of the religious attitude of the Hebrews. The Greek might feel a personal relationship to the local manifestation of deity in his country, city or island; but it was a phase of his patriotism. This could never reach—and did not, in literary expression, ever reach—the depth of feeling that is expressed in the Psalms. Philosophical expressions of such relationship, as in Cleanthes' Hymn, are as colorless as, for us, an ode to the Absolute. It might be thought that the influence and teaching of the Mysteries ( μυστήρια, τελεταί ) would have supplied this lack for Plato as it did for so many Greeks. So it has been held that Plato's general doctrine of the soul and of its relation to the divine with the possibilities in that of ultimate purification was derived from or influenced by the Orphic doctrine. But it is plain that there were aspects of that doctrine which Plato greatly disliked and he appears to have ignored it as much as possible. In the *Laws* there is an allusion to the Orphic prohibition of animal food (782 C). In 870 D it is allowed that there is an emotional weight and sanction given to a moral principle seriously related at these rites as to vengeance in Hades and in a second life, but Plato himself prefers to lay down a law. For such mystic rites ( τελεταί ) may be turned by crafty men to private and personal uses (908 D *ff.*) and may go to foster the idea that the gods are open to bribes. In the *Republic* (364) this is worked out at still greater length. There Plato pro-tests strongly against Orphic mystery-mongers who, without any real morality, deal in magic forms and threats concerning the other world. We have already seen the author of "Wisdom" taking up an even stronger position as to the Mysteries. And so in Plato's *Laws* the feeling of a fostering, protecting, guiding Divinity, which undoubtedly exists there, is either vaguely diffused or split up amongst a number of personal gods. The expression "our King," quoted above, is as far as emotional expression ever gets. The driving force and soul-grappling power in the realization of the personal Jehovah which the Hebrews had are unknown to these speculations. That force had founded a state among the Hebrews closely like to the state visioned in Plato's *Laws,* and nothing else could have done that. And Plato himself was perfectly conscious that such a state as he visioned could be built only on a theocratic basis. He went back for his foundations to the old Greek concep-tions of divinely guided lawgivers—the laws of Crete being derived reputedly from Zeus through Minos and the laws of Lacedaemon being derived from Apollo through Lycurgus—and, so, he speaks of a "lawgiver" much as the Jews gave that name to Moses. The guidance of a god lay behind. And the state, being thus theocratic in basis, could be preserved only by securing that basis under penalties. The Hebrews, so far as they secured their state, did it under the fear of Jehovah. In Plato's state no atheist might be allowed to live, nor anyone who held, as, later, Epicurus (d. 270 B.C.) that the gods took no heed of human affairs; nor any who held, as so many everywhere in varying fashion, that the gods could be bribed. To deal with these, various laws were laid down, but the end for the unrepentant is always death. This part of Plato's scheme was markedly un-Hebrew, as we shall see, and carries us forward to the Geneva of Calvin and the fate of Servetus there. As has often been shown, religious intolerance began with the intellectual arrogance of philosophers who were sure that they were right, and not with theologians. Theologians took the assurance of certainty over from them. How the Nocturnal Council of this state would have dealt with Socrates, and Socrates with it, may be a wide question. It would have been still easier than at Athens to convict him of *incivisme* towards its unchangeable order. Certainly a picture of Socrates wandering about in this last creation of Plato's brain, questioning, talking, exposing, teaching, is of a fantastic impossibility.

The kindly guidance of the gods went into minute details. In pity for the human race in its misery they ordained feasts and taught choric songs and dancing and gave men as companions in these Apollo, the Muses and Dionysus. And these songs and dances once fixed in the right and best form, with fitting tunes and words, must be preserved unchanged in type, as Egyptian art had been kept stereotyped so long (653 *ff.*). In all forms of art the Egyptians from the beginning had been rightly guided and it was to their praise that they had held to the primeval models. This is a startling illustration of the degree to which Plato's mind had come to deify fixed tradition. The revolutionary art of Pheidias and Praxiteles, because it was revolutionary, is silently disapproved. Yet that did not mean approval of everything Egyptian. He could not approve of their sharp business practice, too like that of the Phoenicians (747 C). Similarly for him the chorus with dancing and song was as sacred and unchangeable as the ritual of the Temple for Ben Sira, which he traced back to David, and it had been developed in much the same way.

An almost startling point of coincidence and also of divergence between the ideas of the aged Plato and those of the Hebrews is to be found in the question of the relation of men to God. For what do men exist so far as God is concerned? For what were men created and how does God regard man? We have already seen that the Hebrews were of divided opinion as to this. Some of them held that all the non-human creation existed for the sake of man and that man was, to some degree, a partaker of the divine nature. Others, however, held that all created things were on one level before Jehovah and existed for one purpose, to be a great animated toy with which Jehovah could occupy Himself and amuse Himself. But they, then, differed further as to the place of man in that toy. To these differences we shall have to return.

In two places in the *Laws* Plato uses this idea of man as the toy of God. It is not the created world as a whole which he so regards but mankind alone. Men are the puppets ($\theta a\acute{v}\mu a\tau a$) of God and are pulled by strings as in a puppet-show. In the first passage (644 D *ff.*) it is left obscure as to whether this comparison of men to puppets pulled by strings is only a vivid way of expressing the emotions which rule them in their life under the eyes of the gods or whether it expresses the final reality in the nature of man; that man, whatever the object of the gods might be, was really their puppet. Plato calls this a "myth" ($\mu\hat{v}\theta os$), but he, also, throws out as a way of regarding men that "each of us is a puppet made by the gods, possibly as a plaything, or possibly with some serious purpose ($\sigma\pi ov\delta\hat{\eta}\ \tau\iota v\iota$)—for as to that we know nothing." This suggests that Plato himself was serious in regarding such a conception as a possible explanation of the abiding puzzle of the purpose of life. It pushed the problem back to the inscrutable purpose of God, and for Plato in the *Laws* the divine background of life is overwhelming and man's only true guide and full safety is to follow it and adjust himself to it. Man's chief end is to glorify God and enjoy him forever. Also we may ask whether when Plato calls man a $\theta a\hat{v}\mu a\ \theta\epsilon\hat{\iota}ov$, that means a puppet made by gods or a puppet with something of divinity in it. The strings, however, are our inward affections which drag us along and which pull against one another to opposite actions of goodness and badness. Further, the object of the whole representation is to urge us, with whatever freedom this leaves to us, to cooperate with that especial leading string which is the public law of the state.

The second passage (803 C *ff.*) is much more explicit and even, indeed, half cynical. It throws a curious light upon Plato's feeling, at least now in his old age, as to the dubious value of life. We must never forget that this is a disappointed, disillusioned, Plato, very far from having the free zest for life which Socrates showed even up to his death, when he was of about the same age. Human affairs, we are told, do not deserve to be taken too seriously. Yet man cannot help himself; he must live and that is his misfortune. So he must be serious in the right way and about the right things. And that means God, for man is contrived to be a plaything ( παίγνιον) of God, which is the best thing about man. Apparently the connection is : If the gods play with man, play is serious and worth while, for it is part of the life of the gods. Let man, then, take his play, too, seriously and use it for education and so honor the gods and win their favor and adjust himself to their play and accept his status with them, "being puppets for the most part, but sharing occasionally in truth" ( ἀλήθεια, 804 B), that is, in absolute truth, the reality of the gods. Professor Taylor renders freely, "though with some touch of reality about them, too." And, if we so do, the divine powers will add suggestion and guidance as to things necessary for the service of the gods. It is plain that Plato recognizes that this doctrine of the status of man will shock most people, for twice he makes his interlocutors object. But it is plain, also, that he here expresses his deepest and most intimate sense of the pathetic riddle of life—a puppet-show worked by the gods for their own amusement and yet with something ultimate and divine in the puppets (899 D). The gods are good; their world is rational, just and beautiful. So he partially excuses himself on the ground that in thus describing man he was carried away, in feeling, by the thought of God; struck with "enthusiasm" in the original sense of the Greek ἐνθουσιασμός, divine transport; apparently the vision of the unutterable separation between man and the Divine. Let man, then, he concludes, use his possibility, accept his status, and yield himself to the divine guidance. We have the infinite pathos of a puppet-show in which the puppets are self-conscious and have a certain choice as to which cord they will allow to draw them. It is the old question of external control and free will, and the nearest to this view is the psychological solution worked out by one school of the scholastic theologians of Islam. According to that view man is a pure automaton and his every motion depends upon the eternal and unchanging will of Allah. Man's consciousness of exercising free will in making a choice is only another detail of his automatism. The most that man has in the action is a paradoxical "accepting" of it as his own, and even that "accepting" is part of the machinery of his structure. In this way it is supposed that the justice of Allah in punishing evil deeds and evil doers can be pre-

served. For Plato, man, the puppet, might be pulled this way and
that by cords of emotion, but his personality came in through his
yielding himself to one cord rather than another. Inasmuch as the
influence of both Plato and Aristotle, especially in Neoplatonic
form, was strong on the development of Muslim scholasticism, it
is very possible that there is here actual influence of Plato on
Muslim theology. It was combined there with a scheme of perpetual
re-creation in atomic time which was derived from Indian
speculation.

These Hebrews, however, who came to think of man as part of
an animated toy spread before the eyes of Jehovah and giving Him
joy were following ancestral clues and owed nothing to foreign
influence. The old poetry of the Arabs in their desert life is full of
descriptions, for their own sake, of mountain and plain, of springs
with their surrounding thickets and grass, flowers and plants, of
wadis and the rushing streams in them fed by cloudbursts in the
hills and of all the swarming, multitudinous wild life which went
with these—wild asses, wild cows, gazelles and their offspring, even
insects, buzzing and chirping beside solitary rain-pools in the
desert. To these pictures the Hebrew poets added the all-seeing,
fostering presence of Jehovah, delighting in His work and finding
it good. Thus from the combination of the Arabic poetic visions
and the unique personality of Jehovah we get the One Hundred
and Fourth Psalm and the Speeches of the Lord in Job. But
when the Hebrew thinkers faced the conception of the earth
in all its amplitude and multitude as the toy of Jehovah, with man
in it as only a part of the whole, they were driven of necessity to
find the part played by man in that whole. For the thinkers of this
school man was not the object of the creation, but still he was a
distinct and even discrepant element in it. Wherein lay his difference? On that they went to two extremes. For the Poet who wrote
the Speeches of the Lord in Job, man had become a discord, a false
tone in the harmony as heard by Jehovah, in the picture of nature
as seen by Jehovah. The wild things of the world could do without
him very well; he marred the simplicity of the whole. We have
almost the savage irony of Swift finding the horses in the Land of
the Houyhnhnms far better than men. But, at the other extreme,
man in the One Hundred and Fourth Psalm has become Nature's

voice and priest, and renders back to Jehovah that praise and worship which the dumb creation cannot give; man can speak to God.

But the greatest contrast between the attitude of Plato in the
*Laws* and that of any Hebrew thinker is to be found in the case of
Ecclesiastes. Ecclesiastes was facing life just as was Plato. He, too,
was trying to work out a map of life and a guide through life. But
his thought was of the individual and not of the construction of
any ideal state.—And it is there, too, in fact, that the permanent
value of Plato's book has come to lie.—He was at one with Plato
in that he posited a supernatural background to all existence and in
that he recognized that a man could lead a tolerable life only by
adjusting himself to that background. This background was an
individual, personal being whom he calls God, for convenience as
much as anything. That was the word which everyone used. But
his fundamental separation from Plato came in the character which
he felt compelled to assign to this Being, the maker and ruler of the
world. For Plato, the divine background, whether one or many,
was good, wise, kind. For Ecclesiastes life was good and living
beings could be wise and kind, but that Being behind life was
entirely amoral—wise it might be, terribly wise. Plato seems really
to argue from man's goodness, which he had experienced, to God's
goodness which he had inferred. But for Ecclesiastes the signs of
evil in the rule of the world were too strong to be ignored; there he
could find no sign of moral consideration. And so Plato's argument
was impossible for him. And he could not even follow hints in his
own Sacred Books that God might be of a mixed character, even
as were men. His Absolute had to be absolute indeed and of no
twynature.

In consequence Ecclesiastes never reached Plato's high optimism
and would have criticized it severely. He would have criticized it
not only because it ignored or, on inadequate grounds, brushed
aside the evident evils of the world, but that it also led Plato to
play fast and loose with absolute truth. Plato would lay under
penalty—would absolutely prohibit—any statement that any wicked
men led pleasant lives or that things profitable may be different
from things just (662 B, C). Teaching must leave unseparated the
pleasant and the just so that we may become fixed in the opinion
that the just is always pleasant. Any denial of this is to be reck-

oned shameful and hateful. This Plato admits (663 D) may be fiction but holds that it is a useful fiction. Ecclesiastes would have said that such a fiction was ignoble and that a sense for truth was not in it. He would have resented Plato's implication that any other view sprang from an unjust and evil standpoint. Here and elsewhere calling names and imputing motives seem to be inseparable from the constructing of idealistic states. Ecclesiastes might have brought Plato's position in line with that in his own Book of Proverbs. Plato practically says, Be good and you will be happy, because the gods are good and have willed that (734 D). The Hebrew Book of Proverbs goes only a step further in teaching, Be good and you will be successful—which Plato implicitly holds (743 f.)

So a fundamental difference between Plato and Ecclesiastes lies in their different estimate of the soul. Plato accepts the customary ideas about the gods and Hades, whatever he may have thought of them. But, accepting these, man must accept the fact of the soul; it is the fixed element in life. He tries in Book X to prove it and its nature and hence the gods and their nature. He is thus incurably psychical and spiritual in his attitudes, and believes, in consequence, that good is behind the universe. The army of unalterable law in the skies means for him unfailing justice on the earth. The soul belongs to these heavenly things and man should be optimistic as to it and as to the whole world. So he can brush aside as misunderstandings and corruptions of the divine purpose the evident evils in this lower world. The human soul is the divine thing in man but it may be corrupted. It is for man to honor his soul and keep it uncorrupted (726 ff.).

Ecclesiastes, on the other hand, develops the realistic side of the Hebrew attitude and thinking, and Life is his great reality. The spirit, it is true, comes from God—he uses the story of man's creation in Genesis much as Plato uses the Greek myths—but this spirit is only to give life to man and to the lower animals also, and at death, it is reabsorbed in the reservoir of life, which is God. That is the complete ending for every man and beyond the grave there is nothing. Ecclesiastes is heartily glad of this, for it means a final escape for man. But to Life, and in this he is very Hebrew, his supreme devotion is due. You are in life, he would urge, live it, use it, enjoy it, and avoid God as much as possible. Above all, do nothing that may irritate God; adjust yourself to His ways and His will. Ecclesiastes had no doubt of his own personality; he was a person to himself and could speak with himself and reason with himself and see himself doing these things; but he never calls this personality "soul." He uses that word only for his physical appetites, and that is its primitive Hebrew meaning. His personality was his "I" and he knew that he had a "mind" (he says "my mind" often) which was "rational" and could "reason," and possessed "wisdom"; like all Hebrews he used the same word for "reason" and "wisdom." But he had no word for "soul" in the sense of Plato's *psyche*; the Hebrew word translated "soul" so often in our English version meant for him, and all Hebrews, the lower, physical nature, the appetites, the psyche of Paul. It was used also to express "self" but always with that lower meaning behind it. Ecclesiastes avoids it and uses it only as in ii, 24, "cause his self to get pleasure."

But, for all this, he was perfectly certain of the superhuman background to life and for him, as for Plato, man had to adjust himself to that. Man was utterly in the hand of God and yet man by exercising his free will could irritate God and bring down destruction upon himself. How did God regard man? Was man in any way an amusing puppet-show to God? There is no trace of such an idea in Ecclesiastes, but he must have known that many Hebrews saw the world as God's animated toy. Life, for him, went on "under the sun," but not explicitly in the eye of God. Yet God was behind it. He had arranged, as we have seen, all the events of life in a scheme of opposites, $A$ and not-$A$. This scheme covered every possibility and the events went round in Time, each coming in an "occasion" fitted to receive it, and the opposites balanced each other and cancelled each other out. This cancelling out by an opposite was the only "divine judgment" which Ecclesiastes could see in the world, and it had no moral meaning. God was behind the scheme and if any man, in the exercise of his free will, broke through the scheme, it was the worse for him. So we get the feeling of God, like a gigantic spider, watching man from behind this web of events, not in the least the pleased spectator of the comedy of life. It is a different picture entirely from that of Plato; God is not the master of a show, pulling the strings of human puppets. God is infinitely debased beneath the level of Plato's God or gods, and man in his complete freedom is infinitely exalted above Plato's puppets, even if there is some element of divinity in them. The manliness and integrity of the Hebrew attitude towards Jehovah— as in David, one gentleman to another—has survived even the bitter disillusionment of Ecclesiastes.

But there is a point at which Plato and Ecclesiastes come strangely together. That all things are controlled by God, Plato is certain; that is his theological position. But he cannot help seeing also the facts of life and these are that chance ($\tau\acute{\nu}\chi\eta$) and occasion ($\kappa\alpha\iota\rho\acute{o}s$) and accidents ($\xi\upsilon\mu\phi\rho\alpha\acute{\iota}$) of all kinds control human affairs. He even says that they do so "with God" ($\mu\epsilon\tau\grave{\alpha}\ \theta\epsilon o\hat{\upsilon}$), "cooperate with God in all human affairs," Dr. Bury translates; "under God" as Professor Taylor renders, would surely require grammatically Badham's conjecture $\mu\epsilon\tau\grave{\alpha}\ \theta\epsilon\acute{o}\nu$ but Professor Taylor gives no note of deserting his standard text. Human art or skill ($\tau\acute{\epsilon}\chi\nu\eta$) also plays its part and cooperates with "occasions" (709 A, C). So Plato faces life as he had seen it and leaves his experience in unsolved contrast with his theological theory.

Ecclesiastes, on his side, had no such difficulty for he had no such theory of God's goodness. So when he says (ix, 11) that "occasion and occurrence happen to all men "and that neither wisdom nor understanding nor strength are of any essential avail in life he was only emphasizing his assurance that God went His way regardless of men. Yet the coincidence is curious. Both are looking at the same facts and using almost the same words. "Occasion" is rendered in the Greek version of Ecclesiastes by exactly the same word, $\kappa\alpha\iota\rho\acute{o}s$, and in the Hebrew and in the Greek it is the same word also which is used (iii, 1-8) of the different "occasions" in which the events of life fall. "Occurrence" is a different word from "chance" ($\tau\acute{\nu}\chi\eta$). In the Greek version of Ecclesiastes it is $\dot{\alpha}\pi\acute{\alpha}\nu\tau\eta\mu\alpha$ and the original Hebrew word means "a striking against one"—essentially the idea of chance-medley. Thus for Ecclesiastes man had to find his way through a cunningly but mechanically devised scheme of life in which the best and strongest qualities of human nature were of comparatively little use to him. In the last analysis, as he reiterates through his book, even "wisdom" might be of little help. Plato had a high opinion of human art and skill when it cooperated with "occasion." Ecclesiastes begins his book with the wisdom and skill of Solomon cooperating with his high station and endless resources and finds that it brought nothing but Solomon's own joy in the moment of working. But man must play the game as God had arranged the pieces, yet why God had constructed such a scheme no one could tell and Ecclesiastes never even troubled to ask. He was not interested in God except as a Being to be avoided, but he was tremendously interested in life, because he had to live life. His book was written as a guide to that living and not as a study of the quite inscrutable Being behind it all. Plato would probably have acknowledged that Ecclesiastes' position was a possible statement and interpretation of the facts of experience, but he would, in spite of it, have insisted on clinging to his conception of God as good, wise and kind. Plato was possessed with the idea of God, but Ecclesiastes, in his calm, analytical, balancing way, if he was possessed with anything it was with life. The Book of Ecclesiastes is thus the most thoroughgoing criticism of the basal Platonic position and is a departure from the normal Hebrew position in so far as the character and estimate of Jehovah are concerned. That there was behind life a single all-powerful personality he, of course, never doubted.

Exactly the opposite holds of the Book of Ben Sira, called Ecclesiasticus. Ben Sira lived in the time of the rule of the High Priests in Jerusalem when the administration of the theocracy of Israel had come into the hands of a priestly aristocracy applying, according to its lights, the Levitical legislation. The parallel of this with Plato's state is of the closest. Plato's, too, was an essential theocracy; the gods were considered throughout as the real founders and rulers whose wishes and advice were to be sought in different ways, even by casting lots, as often among the Hebrews, and whose fostering care was assured. By the equality of the lot internal discord might be avoided and this means should be used, praying God and Good Luck ($\dot{\alpha}\gamma\alpha\theta\grave{\eta}$ $\tau\acute{\nu}\chi\eta$) to guide it (757 E). The "lawgiver" to the state appears in many passages in essentially the same position as Moses, between Jehovah and Israel. The state once founded and organized was to be maintained as unchanged as possible; it was a divine foundation and, therefore, peccable only on its human side. Even the supreme Nocturnal Council would have seemed to Ben Sira closely parallel to the Council of the High Priest and Elders which he knew. The penal laws against atheists, Epicureans and bribers of the gods he would have understood, but certainly found over-severe. Israel had never known straight atheists—deniers of a divine background to the world. It had known those who said that God was afar off and took no care of mortal things; but it had contented itself with calling them fools. They were under no other penalty. Attempted bribers of God with sacrifices, Israel had always known. It was the characteristic vice of a sacrificial system and the prophets had protested against it. But Ben Sira knew that so long as there was a professional priesthood it would be corrupted in that way. He, too, protested, as Amos long before had done, and could do no more. The Law and the priesthood were for him the foundation of Israel. So he would have been in thorough sympathy with Plato's insistence on keeping up the traditional sacrificial system (716 D ff. and often). He would have been in sympathy, too, with the strictly supervised and regulated choric songs and dances and would have compared them with the splendid ritual of the Temple which meant so much to him. The object in both cases was the same.

Another point of contact would have been the place assigned to Reason. Ben Sira, as we have seen, was compelled to recognize Reason as an element in the world, but set his face against the conception of it as a Being coeternal with Jehovah, and an independent guide for mankind, working through and in nature and man himself and leading to a natural theology. This conception, as has been shown above, was reached by Hebrew thinkers on an independent basis, starting with the given facts of Jehovah and His revealed law and, above all, with His fear, yet leaving all that far behind. But for Ben Sira this Reason became a created being, a personification of Jehovah in time and space, proceeding from Him, His creative word, to be identified with the Law itself, and a teacher of men. All the being, also, of this Reason, first and last, is the Fear of Jehovah. So Ben Sira tried to save the situation.

This, expressed in very different terms, seems to be closely the place of Reason ( νοῦς ) in Plato's world of the *Laws*. In that world Law ( νόμος ) is deified, but behind Law and the source of

Law is Reason. Reason rules all the motions of the heavens, and the mathematician who can trace out those movements and realize their inerrancy knows of a certainty that there is reason in them and behind them, that the gods possess reason and rule in reason. But the gods are good and reason is part of their goodness, as it is part of human goodness (900 D), although men, with mortal eyes, can never behold and know reason fully (897 D). There is no law mightier than knowledge ($\dot{\epsilon}\pi\iota\sigma\tau\dot{\eta}\mu\eta$) and reason ($\nu o\hat{\upsilon}s$) is lord of all things. That is the ideal position, but for man there must be ordinances and laws (875 C, D). Reason, then, is of the divine nature and the laws divinely appointed for men are a dispensation, or largess, on the part of reason ($\nu o\hat{\upsilon}$ $\delta\iota\alpha\nu o\mu\dot{\eta}$). Reason and virtue are the same, for virtue consists of four things and reason is the chief of these (963 A).

Ben Sira and Plato reached these similar positions along the most diverse roads and expressed them in the most dissimilar language. But common to them both and distinguishing both from the position that Reason is a coeternal with God, reached in Proverbs viii, is the position that Reason is the possession of God and not an entity separate, or separable, from God. Perhaps Ben Sira may have personified Reason more than Plato, or, perhaps, his personifying was due to the genius of the Hebrew language. In Plato the pursuit of pure reason is open to men only in the higher mathematics and when a man has penetrated these mysteries he finds that reason is the thinking of God. Ben Sira takes no account of mathematics, but his Reason is the creative word of Jehovah, meeting men and teaching them in and through all the operations of the world.

There are other little, nonphilosophical, coincidences between the two schemes; e.g. the attempt to secure and perpetuate a certain number of families and certain landed holdings. In Plato's state the number of 5040 hearths must be preserved, no more, no less. Under divine penalty these cannot be bought or sold (740 *ff.*; 746 *ff.*; 843 *ff.*). This is very similar to the Levitical legislation to preserve the possessions of the families and the tribes. Ben Sira would have recognized at once that it aimed at a Hebrew ideal.

So Ben Sira would have felt much attracted to this dream of Plato's if he had ever known it. His great difficulty would have lain in Plato's indifference as to monotheism. He himself had no use even for angels; in his complete spiritual monism his Unseen World consisted of Jehovah alone. But he must have known of the historical development by which the Elohím and Sons of Elohím had been cleared away out of Hebrew thought until Jehovah had absorbed them all into Himself and was one single personality occupying the whole spiritual world. He would have a certain amount of sympathy, then, with Plato's indeterminate position between "God" and "the God" and "the gods" and all the daemons and heroes. A single mental motion would have reduced to nullity all these unnecessary deities and left God alone in His wisdom and kindness and love to rule the world and guide the souls of men. But for Plato's mind that single motion would have rendered still more impossible his new state by destroying its connection with the old Greek hereditary pieties, observances and associations; the very basis of it all in ancient fear and reverence would have gone.

So that was not to be and the Neoplatonists were to destroy the religious value of Platonism by removing Plato's God to metaphysical and unknowable aloofness and by holding fast to the multiplicity of daemons. The Neoplatonic Chain might be called the exact opposite of the immediate presence and working of the personal Jehovah in the world. It is almost as opposed to the relation which Plato himself had reached with his God.

All this we can imagine Ben Sira thinking if he had ever come to know this ideal state which Plato had sketched a century and a half before his time. It would be amusing to attempt to write an anachronistic "imaginary conversation" between those three, Plato, Ben Sira and Ecclesiastes. Ecclesiastes would have to play much the part of Socrates, the keen questioner, the doubter and gentle refuter. For he had Socrates' sense of the reality and value of life, his devotion to the facts of life and his integrity of thought. As for Ben Sira and Plato, very little—after the great step of clearing away the litter of subordinate gods—separated them, except names and words. These two old men, by the most different paths, had come to similar ideals. Experiences and circumstances had overcome diversity of starting points. With them, thus face to face, this consideration and vindication of the Hebrew philosophical life may fitly close. The Hebrews had always been Platonists and now the old age of their thinking came together with the old age of Plato's.

# EPILOGUE

APART from the vindication of the philosophical genius of the Hebrews, it has been an object of this book to draw attention to a thread of derivation and development of Trinitarian doctrine which is too often neglected. Theological doctrines as they form in the human mind are but adumbrations of divine realities and they are reached gradually and along often surprising paths.

All revelation centers round that supreme divine Reality which we call God, and all theological doctrines are approximations to a description of that final Reality. In their consideration of the world and of themselves the Hebrews reached the concept of Reason and they personified that concept, as their manner was. It was a reality to them and it became a Person. They were then met with the problem of adjusting this Reason to the primary and basal personality of Jehovah. Both their philosophical and theological instincts recoiled before the positing of two coequal and coeternal primary Realities. Of long inheritance, but also very subtly, they had in them the instinct of monism—the necessity for a primary unity. But they had also learned to separate out Reason as one of the governing and guiding principles of life and in life. They knew it in themselves. Reason had become a tremendous reality to them. They found Reason, too, teaching her children in all the phases of the world around them; she belonged to the primary structure of all existence. So they became as devoted to Reason, viewed in this absolute, metaphysical way, as were any Greeks. And many of them were plainly unwilling to say that this Reason in the structure of things was only a quality in God just as there was reason in each man; that as man was rational, so God was rational; and that that was all reason meant. Some, even, held that in the pursuit of Reason you did not need to begin with Jehovah. The first step in getting Reason was simply getting Reason and Reason was eager to be found by man. Whatever the relation of men might be to God, by their very created nature they were the sons of Reason. The problem, then, dealt not with an abstract idea but with the whole background of life and also in the end with the personality of Jehovah.

Thus the problem was present and serious. The Hebrews never had the slightest intention, however philosophical they might be, of turning from Jehovah and giving themselves to pure Reason. The conception of a personality behind existence had become part of their blood and bone. Jehovah, the God of their fathers, might be turned, on the evidence of the facts of the world, into an entirely amoral Being, but He was still the final Reality of all, the Absolute for them. So Ecclesiastes found Him and left Him; and at the same time minimized reason. But those who had seen Her glory and beauty and had become Her worshipers had to find some relation between this evident deity and Jehovah.

The poet who wrote that strange little poem, which now forms the twenty-eighth chapter of our Book of Job, describes how Jehovah found her at the back of Creation, considered her and kept her for Himself. What that poet meant by this on the positive side, we can only guess; negatively he meant that man does not possess this absolute Reason. Some, probably much more pious, were willing to admit that man might possess her, but only through fearing Jehovah. Otherwise man was condemned to abiding foolishness.

Apart from these very tentative and inadequate solutions we have seen above three great attacks on the problem, those of Ben Sira, of the author of the Book of Wisdom and of the author of the Fourth Gospel. Ben Sira plainly had no liking for the idea but was compelled to face it by its evident popularity in his time. It is much against his will that he philosophizes even so far as he goes. And so he weaves the idea into the imagery of the tabernacle and of the ritual—dealing on the part of Jehovah with His people. Round the ceremonial of the tabernacle and the Temple all Ben Sira's ideas centered, and he turns this Reason into the soul, or spirit, of that ceremonial. Through her, in the name of Jehovah, the Levitical dispensation spoke to the people. And through her Jehovah Himself manifested Himself to the people; she is the executive and revealing word from His mouth. The older Scriptures were full of phrases how the word of Jehovah came to this one and that one; she in a supreme and universal sense was that Word.

The author of the Book of Wisdom took an entirely different course. The Levitical ceremonial meant nothing to him and the Mosaic legislation almost nothing. The omnipotent, righteous, true and loving personality of Jehovah—the Lord—was everything. And this "Wisdom" is a unique personality who manifests Him to all mankind. Perhaps the nearest to this conception in our Christian theology is "the Holy Ghost, the Lord, and Giver of life, who proceedeth from the Father." There are many differences, but that was the broad direction in which the Hebrew Reason was developing at the hands of this thinker. And the development was going on under the stress and guidance of all the Greek philosophies current at Alexandria.

The third solution was formed by Christian theology and has remained an essential element in it. There the conception is boldly taken up into the description of God Himself and has become the philosophical foundation of the doctrine of the Trinity. The author of our Fourth Gospel completely accepted that view of the personality of Christ which recorded Him as the Reason described in the eighth chapter of Proverbs, but now incarnate and visible and speaking immediately to men. The whole position of the philosopher in Proverbs was taken over and developed as Christian verity. This Reason was from the beginning, was the creator of the world and was God. This Reason was also the Light and guide of all men of all times and races. Now that Reason had been manifested in Jesus Christ and all had seen Him. There are suggestions of this view in other Gospel strands of tradition, but the Fourth Gospel is given to its complete development and only as so interpreted is that Gospel plain. See further on this *The Hebrew Literary Genius,* pp. 187 *ff.*

There was an interesting parallel about three centuries later to this remoulding of an old religion under foreign influences. The authors of the Hermetic writings, to which allusion has been made several times above, evidently began from primitive Egyptian religion, or, rather, religiosity, just as the Hebrews began from the religion of Jehovah. This primitive religion was then enormously modified by the influence of later Greek philosophy—Platonism, Stoicism and various syncretisms. The Jewish parallel to this is the system of the Book of Wisdom. But there is one great difference.

The essential in the character of Jehovah remains unaffected in the Book of Wisdom; it is the nonessentials which drop away. And the philosophical influences serve only to develop, illustrate and make intelligible that essential character to other racial types of mind. The Hermetists, on the other hand, completely transformed their conception of the divine nature. What they preserved was the religiosity of the Egyptian mind. They were also affected by speculations freely built on the Book of Genesis and, to a less degree, by Christian conceptions. It would be curious and instructive to compare and contrast the history of modification and transformation in their case with that through which the Hebrews went. But even now it is plain how perfectly the character and personality of Jehovah as conceived by the Hebrews stood this strain.

# INDEX OF SCRIPTURE REFERENCES
## WITH SOME OTHERS

The references to Greek philosophy are not listed because they are not handled
—except, perhaps, in the last chapter—as primary, but as illustrative, for comparison and contrast. The references to Philo, Clement of Alexandria, and the
Hermetica, on the other hand, are primary, so far as they go.